Scrum for Teams

Scrum for Teams

A Guide by Practical Example

Dion Nicolaas

 BUSINESS EXPERT PRESS

First published in 2018 by
Business Expert Press, LLC
222 East 46th Street, New York, NY 10017
www.businessexpertpress.com

ISBN-13: 978-1-94819-843-1 (paperback)
ISBN-13: 978-1-94819-844-8 (e-book)

Business Expert Press Portfolio and Project Management Collection

Collection ISSN: 2156-8189 (print)
Collection ISSN: 2156-8200 (electronic)

Cover and interior design by S4Carlisle Publishing Services Private Ltd., Chennai, India

First edition: 2018

10 9 8 7 6 5 4 3 2 1

Printed in the United States of America.

Abstract

Scrum is an agile framework for completing complex projects.

This book gives examples, tools, and tricks to do Scrum well. For each trick it is explained why it helps. The practices themselves may be worth trying, but by understanding why it works the readers will be able to come up with their own ideas that work better in their organization and situation.

All the practical examples in this book have helped someone, somewhere to become a part of a better Scrum team. Scrum's motto is: "Inspect and Adapt"; change small things one at a time and see what works.

Scrum is not done by project leaders or managers, but really by the teams—to succeed in an organization, the teams must do Scrum well. If the teams do Scrum well, the whole organization will benefit from it.

Scrum helps teams self-organize, which fits in well with developers, who usually don't like to be micromanaged. At the same time, Scrum can scale: Self-organized teams work together well, and one manager doesn't have to manage all the people.

The lessons from this book help Scrum teams develop into autonomous, proud, and independent teams. Often teams fail to become powerful enough to change the organization, so they cannot perform to their full potential. A good team can lead the stakeholders into trusting them. They will then make plans based on the team's release planning instead of making roadmaps out of thin air, and thus make the organization much more predictable.

Who Is the Audience for This Book and Why Would They Buy It?

- Members of Scrum teams, to learn how to become good at Scrum
- People involved in delivering or managing complex projects, to learn an agile way to do that
- Students studying project and program management

Keywords

agile, change management, complex projects, management, practical guide, scrum, self-organization, software development, teamwork, tips and tools

Contents

Preface

When Jeff Sutherland taught his Certified Scrum Master course, I was most impressed by how he answered all questions: by giving an example of a team somewhere that had the same problem, and solved it in this or that way. I think Scrum should be taught that way: by example. There may be a lot of theory as to how to have people work together on large and difficult work; but it requires a lot of practice.

This is *Scrum for Teams: A Guide by Practical Example*. I've been working with Scrum for over a decade now and found out it is not easy to do it right.

But once a team does get it right, it is a very rewarding experience. The team turns into a team with a purpose: delivering products in the best possible way. Individual team members help each other, make each other better, and become better. The team becomes proud, autonomous, and efficient.

And when the organization the team belongs to understands what is happening and supports it, the whole organization benefits from the team, and the other teams that work well. Collaboration between teams becomes natural, communication lines are short, and the whole organization moves forward in an organic but organized way.

But most importantly, I see that developers *like* Scrum. They feel happy and free in a team that is getting the best out of everyone. That's why I want Scrum to work well.

So here are my examples, tools, and tricks to do Scrum well. All teams are different; what worked for me might not work for you. But every example has helped someone, somewhere to become a better Scrum team, so every story might be helpful to you too.

Acknowledgments

The first time I heard of Scrum was when Jeroen van Eekelen introduced it in our department at TomTom International BV, and he sent me to the Scrum Master course. Two days with Jeff Sutherland made me think that this could work. I wanted to try this with my team and with other teams in the company.

We started experimenting and went through a lot of growing pains. But we enjoyed it and learned a lot along the way. I decided to write down the lessons learned, so we wouldn't forget; and I wanted others to benefit from them too. I started teaching Scrum to other teams at TomTom International BV, which I do to date. I learned a lot from those teams too: trying to solve others' problems often helps you to see your own short-comings more clearly.

I wouldn't have started this if it wasn't for Simon Reason, who is the best Scrum Master we ever had. He taught us how to do Scrum. He was also the first one to read this and provide me with lots of useful comments. I owe a lot to Simon for that; thank you, Simon.

The idea that this could be a real book came from the people from The Pragmatic Bookshelf. I want to thank them for giving me the freedom to publish this book myself. Special thanks go to Jackie Carter, for being critical and encouraging at the same time.

The proofreaders were very helpful; they made me feel it was worthwhile to go on with it. Thanks to Tim Ottinger, Jeff Langr, Robert Shaw, Henk Jan Huizer, Lasse Koskela, Johanna Rothman, Wouter Lagerweij, and Venkat Subramaniam, for your constructive and detailed feedback.

I want to thank Nigel Wyatt for finding the opportunity with Business Expert Press. Thanks to Tim Kloppenborg for his useful suggestions; you really made this a better book. Thanks to Scott Isenberg, Charlene Kronstedt, Kiruthigadevi Nirmaladevi, and the S4 Carlisle team for turning this into a real book. There is a lot more to books than just writing; I'm delighted about how it all came together.

Writing books is bad for families. My kids Hanna, Piter, and Brechtje always make me feel good by being interested in what I do. Anke Petra made sure it didn't all fall apart, indulged with evenings spent working, and sent me to bed at night so I was able to get up in the morning. Home is where my love is.

A big "thank you" goes of course to the Scrum teams I've been working with at TomTom International BV. I learned everything from you, guys'n'gals. This book wouldn't be a guide by practical example without you. In theory, there is no difference between theory and practice, but in practice . . .

CHAPTER 1

Introduction

I'd like to introduce you to The Team. I don't know why they started doing Scrum: maybe the management heard of *agile* and thought it was a good idea; maybe their project manager got enthusiastic about this new way of managing projects during a conference; maybe they decided themselves that they wanted to jump onto the agile bandwagon. But anyway, they started doing stand-up meetings, fixed-length sprints and sprint planning meetings. Their colleagues made funny faces when they gathered around their Scrum board and had their short meetings. Their stakeholders mumbled in their beards when they said they couldn't change the planning for another two weeks. But they did Scrum! And it worked: they delivered some really nice new features after their first iteration, and got encouraged to proceed on the chosen path.

But after a few sprints, the spirit started to wane. Stand-up meetings started late or were skipped altogether, sprints lasted longer than originally decided, and the team slipped back into old habits. "After all," they said, "Scrum is not a *method*, it's a *template*! Which means you can change it!" So The Team changed the template to fit in more and more with their old way of working, until someone realized they weren't doing Scrum anymore. And then they decided that Scrum really wasn't working for them. So they moved on, to PRINCE2, or KanBan, or RUP, and we lose track of them. Maybe they serve as an example in another book; The Team is a very common phenomenon.

The Team is us, of course, when we just started to do Scrum. But we didn't decide that Scrum wasn't working for us; instead, we decided we wanted to make this work. We went back to the basics and tried again.

We kept on going back to the basics, trying to make it work. And we got better! With each and every sprint, we gained some experience, we learned something new, until we could finally say with a straight face that we were doing Scrum.

The Team is also other teams I've been part of, as Scrum Master, Product Owner, or team member. Each team needs to work out for themselves how they can make Scrum work for them. Some problems are encountered by a lot of teams and some are very special. But in each Scrum team I've been, I've learned something.

Maybe you are doing Scrum and you go through all the moves; perhaps you are even a Certified Scrum Master . . . but still you're waiting for that mythical state of hyperproductivity. Even though you know how to *do* Scrum, it doesn't really *work*. You're getting along, but you ask yourself what the hype is about.

A problem with Scrum is that there is so little of it. There is not a lot to change if you want to do Scrum: a few roles, a few meetings, and you're doing it. That can feel unsatisfying, so some teams start to add their own bits from the start. But if they do that before they understand the essence of Scrum, they will probably never get it right.

For Scrum to work for you, you must do it properly until it clicks. After a while, everything will fall in place and you suddenly see why you do stand-ups, why you need a Scrum board, or why story points are a good idea. But you need a little patience for that to happen. Scrum probably doesn't give you much after one sprint. But after four or five sprints, you should start seeing the difference.

But Scrum needs to be understood by the team. Even with full management support in an agile organization, Scrum may fail if the team is not getting it right. And even if the team is completely on their own, they can be fairly successful at Scrum if they know how to do it. Scrum is done by teams. This book helps the team to become good at it.

Not every Scrum team will need to learn everything in this book in order, although it probably won't hurt to read all the chapters. Some teams might be doing well in some areas but not so good in others. Some teams might get almost everything right but lack in one little detail. Learn from this book in priority order: Discuss with the entire team what hurts the most, read the corresponding chapter, and pick the advice you think is most useful. Pick two or three things at a time and pay attention to them during a sprint. Discuss them in a retrospective meeting: Did it work? Is it better now? Follow more advice, until you feel something has changed. Then move on to the next.

Scrum is hard. Even though the methodology, or the template, is easy enough, doing it right requires a lot of attention. It can take a team months to get it more or less right; some teams never get it. And when it doesn't pay off, it becomes a burden. That is the moment that teams decide that "Scrum isn't for them" or "Scrum doesn't work." Indeed, something that slows you down can better be ditched. But even better is to make it work for you.

CHAPTER 2

What Is Scrum?

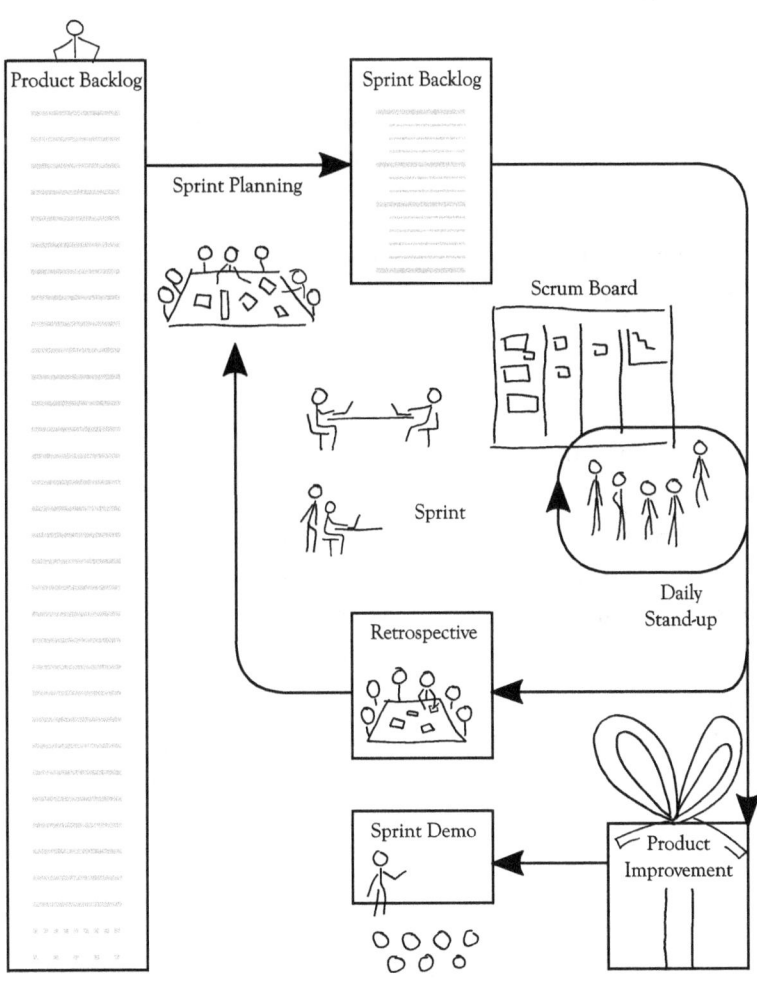

Figure 2.1 The Scrum process

Scrum is an agile framework for managing projects. What does that mean?

It is agile:

> The process is lightweight and flexible.

It is a framework:

> Scrum gives a clear structure to agile practices; that makes it ideal to get started with agile development.

It is iterative:

> The work to be done is chopped up in pieces and done in equal periods of time, reducing complexity and giving a clear view on progress.

Scrum was inspired by the lean manufacturing practices in use by Toyota. Jeff Sutherland and Ken Schwaber presented the Scrum methodology in 1995.

Scrum is really simple. The driving principle is that you should do product development feature by feature in small, equal-sized iterations, called *sprints* in Scrum. That allows you to work on the most important thing all the time, to stop whenever you've done enough, and to measure your progress. All of these reduce the development time of a project and the risk involved.

Scrum introduces roles, meetings, and artifacts to add some structure to this principle. That way it provides a framework to organize your project. All you have to do is fill it in with your product ideas, your expertise, and, most important of all, your people.

2.1   The Product

A company has a vision, a product they would like to create. Or maybe they have a customer that wants some new features. That's where it starts. They have a team of people that are going to do the work.

Figure 2.1 shows the Scrum process. It shows the roles, meetings, and artifacts that you use in Scrum to organize the project.

2.1.1 The Product Owner

The *Product Owner* owns the product vision. He or she needs to share the vision with the rest of the Scrum team, so that they can make it into a real product.

The Product Owner can be the real stakeholder for the features, but it can also be that he or she represents the customer. Either way, the Product Owner needs to know exactly what the final product should do. If someone in the team has questions about how things should work, the Product Owner must answer them. If the team comes up with an interesting idea to do something, the Product Owner must be able to decide whether it is valuable. The Product Owner is the link between the team and the stakeholders.

2.1.2 The Product Backlog

To help the team understand what they need to do, the Product Owner chops the product up into bite-sized chunks: single features that can be created by the team in less than a week. Often these features are written in the form of user stories. The complete list of user stories is called the *product backlog.*

The Product Owner orders the product backlog by business value: User stories yielding the highest return of investment come first. Now if the team works on the product backlog from the top down, the most important features are done first.

2.2 The Process

Once the product backlog is there, the process can start.

2.2.1 The Scrum Master

If the product backlog is ready, the team can start working on the product. They follow a simple work process, which the *Scrum Master* leads.

2.2.2 The Sprint Planning

Together with the Scrum Master, the Product Owner organizes a *sprint planning* meeting with the team. The Scrum Master chairs the meeting where the Product Owner presents the product backlog to the team.

2.2.3 The Sprint Backlog

The goal of the meeting is to decide on a *sprint backlog*: a list of user stories that the team thinks they can do in a fixed period of time (usually 2 to 4 weeks). That period is called a *sprint*.

The team decides what they can do. The Product Owner just sets the priorities. But if the team decides they can do a certain amount of work, they commit to that, so that the Product Owner knows what to expect.

2.2.4 The Sprint and the Stand-Up Meeting

Now the team starts the sprint. Each day, they have a *stand-up meeting*: a very short meeting (at most 15 minutes) where they align their work. The team members discuss what they did yesterday, what they will do today, and whether there is anything blocking from doing their work, so-called impediments.

The Scrum Master is responsible for removing the impediments. While the team does everything that is necessary to implement the user stories, the Scrum Master does everything that is necessary to let the team do their work. The Scrum Master owns the process; he or she makes sure the team can work as well as possible.

2.2.5 The Scrum Board

During the sprint, the team uses a *Scrum board* to keep track of their progress. On the Scrum board there are three columns, labeled *To Do*, *In Progress*, and *Done*. Initially, all the work that needs to be done in the sprint is placed in the To Do column, in priority order from top to bottom. As the sprint progresses, items move from To Do to Done.

The Scrum board usually also has a *burn-down chart,* in which the amount of work still to be done is plotted against the time. But a lot more can go onto the Scrum board . . .

2.2.6 The Sprint Demo

At the end of the sprint the team delivers the features they created, the implementation of the user stories. They organize a *sprint demo,* where they demonstrate all the finished user stories. Everybody is invited to the sprint demo: the customer, the stakeholders, the managers, other teams, and anybody else who wants to know what's going on.

The team owns the delivery. They determine the size of the work to be done, commit to the sprint backlog, and do the work necessary to implement the user stories.

2.2.7 The Retrospective Meeting

To optimize their performance, the team holds a *retrospective meeting* after each sprint. A retrospective is a meeting in which the team evaluates the past sprint. Its main focus is on the process, not on the things produced: What went well during the sprint, what problems did you face, and how can you improve the process for the next sprint?

2.3   Measuring Progress

After one or more sprints, the *velocity* of the team will become clear: the amount of work the team can do in a sprint. The Product Owner can use this number to create a *release burn-down,* which will show which features can be delivered by what date.

2.4   Summary

And that's it! Now you know what Scrum is. To summarize it in the shortest possible way: Let the Product Owner split your project into small bits of work, split your time into small sprints, and let your small teams perform their work. Have the Scrum Master guide the process.

Use a couple of simple tools to keep track of where you are, and evaluate regularly how you are doing.

This is the framework the rest of the book is about. Maybe you know it already; this introduction is mainly a reminder and a way to explain the terminology used in the book.

CHAPTER 3

Make the Most of Stand-Ups

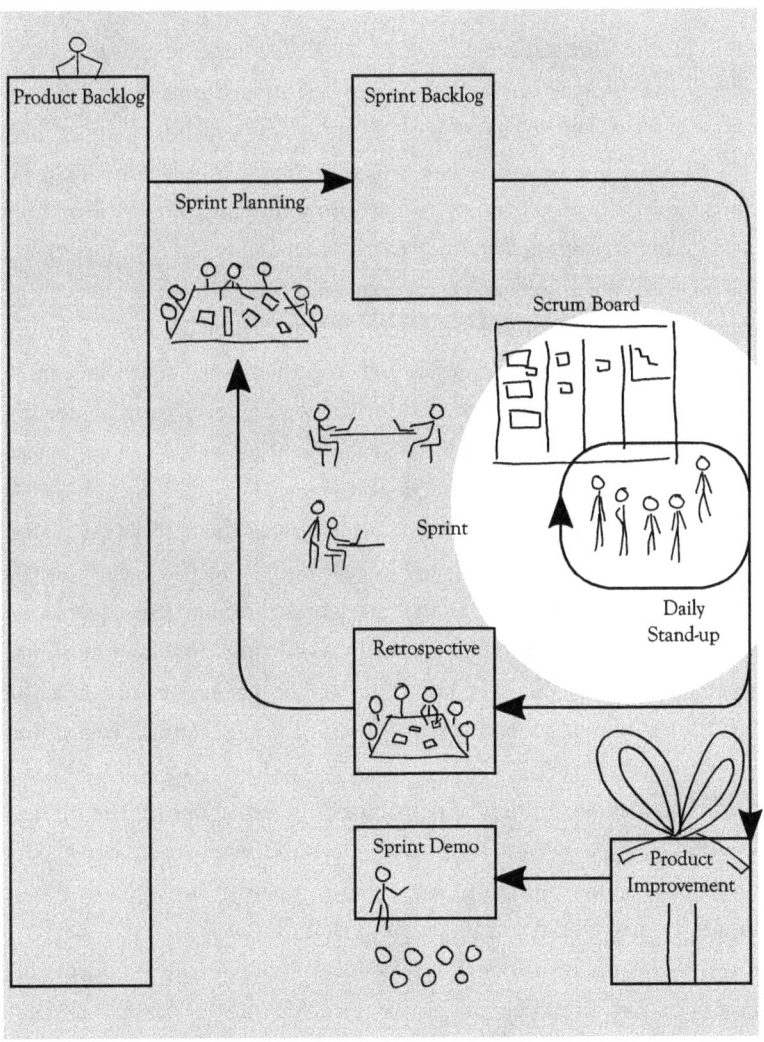

Figure 3.1 The daily stand-up

"Hey, shouldn't we have a stand-up?"

"Well, you know what I'm doing right now, don't you?"

"Wait a second, this is a very complex bit. Can we do it in half an hour?"

"Where's Jennifer?" "She's in another meeting."

"And Chris?" "He's not in yet. It's only ten o'clock!"

At TomTom International BV, I'm an ERO, an emergency response officer. That means I can do first aid and basic firefighting. So far the most exciting things I've done is evacuation trainings (which is pretty exciting in 10-story building with over a thousand people in it—fortunately, I'm not alone). Till today I was not needed for something serious, thankfully.

I do go to a refresher training twice a year and heard this story from a trainer once. When the fire department was fighting a fire in a big building, evacuating people, and trying to extinguish the flames and save the building from collapsing, they would stop their work and have a quick meeting *every hour*. Not everybody would be always in that meeting, because firefighters who had entered the building would not come back for it, but the rest had these frequent meetings.

They needed to discuss the situation as it was then, adapt the plan to any changes or make a new plan, and generally made sure that everyone was aligned about the plan, so that every firefighter understood what was expected from them. It might seem silly to take the time for a meeting if you have to act fast, but if you think about it, it makes sense to take a little bit of time every now and then instead of having everyone run around like headless chickens.

What they were doing was part of *crisis management*. The pressure was high, the stakes were high, so they made sure they were not making mistakes by communicating clearly and frequently. But if that is a good idea in a crisis, wouldn't it be always a good idea?

That's where the daily stand-up comes in. It is perhaps the most visible part of Scrum. Every day the team gathers around the Scrum board and has a short meeting *standing up*. Some call it the daily Scrum. You can see it highlighted in Figure 3.1.

For a team to work together, each member must know what every other member is doing. And not just have a general idea what they are doing, but know it fairly precisely. That way, you can help each other, you don't do double work, and you don't do work that isn't necessary.

A stand-up will help you achieve that; at least that's the textbook theory. But are your stand-ups effective? Do you feel it is working for you?

3.1   Guard Your Time

A fairly common sight: six people standing in front of a Scrum board, waiting for the seventh to arrive. After five minutes, the team is complete and the stand-up can start. But ten minutes later, Gary, the Product Owner, leaves for another meeting . . .

Some people complain that Scrum has too many meetings. Especially the stand-up meeting, which is held every day, is a thorn in their flesh. But it only becomes that when the stand-up meeting is not effective.

An important aspect of effective meetings is to guard the time, both at the start of the meeting and at the end. That means you have to pay attention all the way through.

Starting late makes a lot of people wait, that's one thing. But running late is also not effective.

3.1.1 Start on Time

If you have a very short meeting, it *must* start on time. If you don't, you can never end on time. But shouldn't you wait until everybody is there before you start the meeting? Although that seems obvious, you now run into a problem: People will leave early because the meeting is running late. Usually, people leaving early cause more disruption than people arriving late. When you're leaving early, you often have a good reason: another meeting, an appointment, something to prepare, or something to finish. But arriving late is your fault, so you will try to sneak in and not draw too much attention.

There is another reason to always start on time: People will get used to meetings starting late and will not bother to come on time if that means that they will have to wait. But luckily, people will also get used to meetings starting sharply on time. Starting on time is a habit that will reinforce itself; after some time, nobody will dare to come late anymore.

So start on time—always. Even if only half the group is there, just get it going; let latecomers keep their quiet and not interrupt the meeting. Fill them in later, if they missed something important, and use the opportunity to ask them to be in time next time. In a few days you will all be used to starting on time.

3.1.2 Don't Run Late

Sometimes stand-up meetings take longer than 15 minutes. It's hard to concentrate that long; people start to look around or out of the window; some people might sit down. The subject of the meeting becomes fuzzy. It has become an open-ended meeting that does not result in action items or information exchange.

Don't let that happen. A good stand-up meeting never runs late. It doesn't have to. The key is to realize what a stand-up is all about: to make the whole team aware of what everyone in the team is doing. Not less, because this certainly is a lot to talk about, but not more either. So the Scrum Master should end the meeting after 15 minutes, no matter what. It may seem strange at first, if you're not finished yet, but next time everybody will try harder to keep it short. As the sprint progresses, stand-up meetings can become shorter and shorter.

3.2   Stay on Topic

". . . Now what did I do yesterday? . . ."

". . . I've just gotten in and haven't had time to work out what I will be doing today . . ."

". . . But I really think we should use the Double-checked Locking design pattern in that Singleton, because . . ."

If your meeting is only 15 minutes long, you have to restrict yourselves rigorously. That is why a stand-up meeting has a set agenda: Everybody should know what is expected from them.

3.2.1 Stick to the Three Questions

The three questions that the team members answer in a stand-up meeting are:

1. What did I do yesterday?
2. What will I do today?
3. What are my impediments?

It often happens that the team starts *discussing* those items instead of just listening to them. Although a small amount of discussion can be useful to clarify what's done or going to be done, take your longer discussions outside the meeting. A simple "shall we discuss this after the meeting?" will do. Probably not everyone wants to be in that follow-up meeting.

A stand-up meeting is meant to note what's going on, not to solve it. If necessary, the Scrum Master can keep a list of all things that need to be discussed after the meeting, so that you don't forget.

3.2.2 Be Prepared

Don't waste other people's time trying to work out what you are going to say. Make sure you know your answers to the three questions. Don't go into unnecessary detail though. Come up with the answers that the rest of the team is interested in.

If you know what you are going to say it will also be easier to listen to others. You don't have to search your memory while they are talking.

If it is really hard to remember what you did yesterday, something else is going on. You probably worked on things that were not in the sprint or you were working on many things in parallel. If this happens a lot, this requires investigation: Are your stories too big or too small? Is there enough work in the sprint? That would be a good topic for the retrospective.

3.2.3 The Talking Stick

Order, Order, No Orders

- Have an orderly meeting.
- Speak in logical order.
- Don't give orders.

To have orderly stand-up meetings, it might help to use a token, such as a stick, a pen, or a ball (any ball will do, from a small rugby ball to a large beach ball.) The person who holds the token may speak; everybody else must shut up and listen. Anybody can *request* the token, of course, but the person holding it will pass it on when he or she is done talking.

The token is used as a *talking stick*. Talking sticks were used by North American Indians in tribal councils. Stephen Covey explained how they can be used in modern offices as well in *The 8th Habit*.

The stick is useful in another way: The team member who is done should pass it on to the next logical person. That can be the one he teamed up with or the one who works on the same user story. When the team speaks in logical order, it is easier to understand what's being discussed.

When you use the talking stick, it will be clear when the meeting is over: when everybody has had it. If you want to speak a "parting word" (e.g., because it's your birthday and you brought cake) you can always request the stick one more time at the end.

3.3   Explain Clearly, Listen Carefully

The stand-up begins, and the Sam, the Scrum Master, sets it off.

"You!"

He points to Chris. Chris startles, a bit set off by the command.

". . . Eeh, yesterday . . . Yesterday. Ah, I remember!"

Chris goes on telling to the Scrum Master what he did. Sam waits until he's done, and then points to Laura: "You!"

3.3.1 Talk to the Team

One particular pitfall that should be avoided in stand-up meetings is the Scrum Master asking the next person to speak. A stand-up isn't a status report to the Scrum Master; it is a meeting for the team to align their work.

So when you are speaking, you should address the whole team. The Scrum Master doesn't have to say anything, unless he or she wants to talk about impediments, or demo preparations, or other things that he or she did for the team. The Scrum Master is not the team's leader or manager; the Scrum Master is the team's helper.

The talking stick will help here too. Using the stick the team will structure the meeting themselves, so the Scrum Master can stay more in the background.

3.3.2 Make the Team Understand

Sometimes a team member stands in front of the Scrum board with their back to the rest of the team, moving sticky notes and telling *the board* what they did. This can make it hard for the others to understand what he or she is talking about. Again, you need to speak to the team. If team members find it hard to concentrate on the board and the team at the same time, the team could agree not to move or touch any sticky notes during the stand-up meeting. Or the team members make all their changes to the board at once at the beginning of the stand-up and only then start with the three questions.

Instead of saying "I did this one, and that one, and today I'll take on this one," try to really describe the task. That way you make it as easy as possible for the others to understand you.

Meeting by Phone

Accept this: It is very difficult to have a stand-up meeting with a distributed team. If it is hard to have an effective meeting when you meet in person, it is even harder to do when half of the team is inside a little electronic box on the table. Video conferencing is easier, but still some extra caution is necessary.

Some tips when doing a stand-up meeting by phone:

- Don't gather around the phone and talk to it; gather around the board as usual, and have the phone "participate" just like another team member.
- Talk to the team, not to the phone. The people around you are as important as the people on the other side of the line.
- Starting on time is vital. Phone conferences can feel very vague and ineffective if people come and go.
- It is even more important to be prepared when you meet by phone. When you meet in person and somebody struggles to remember, you can see that and make a joke about it. When it happens over the phone, you miss the visual clue and it is much more irritating.
- Describing the tasks you worked on is really necessary, as people in other places cannot easily see what you are pointing to.

You should try to get the same quick and clear communication going in the phone meeting as in a face-to-face meeting. It should probably even be better, as you have much less chance to talk to each other during the day. And never forget that there is nothing like meeting in person.

3.3.3 Listen, Understand, Remember

What is the hardest part of stand-up meetings? When another team member is speaking, listen to what he or she says. Don't just hear the words: Listen, understand, remember. If you cannot explain after the meeting what everyone is working on, the meeting didn't meet its purpose.

If you don't understand what someone is talking about, ask to clarify it. If you still don't understand, but everybody else seems to understand it, ask for a little extra time after the meeting for more explanation.

Why is this so important? It's not just to be polite. To work together as a team, you can't expect other team members to do their mystery bits while you are doing yours. After all, it will all have to fit together in the end. So to understand the whole picture, to save people from doing double work, and to prevent people from doing useless work, the whole team will have to be involved.

Note that it is *hard* to listen that well. In the beginning, you will not understand everything. You'll have to ask for clarification often. But over time, it will become easier, since everyone in the team is learning.

Walking the Board

In a team, stand-up meetings were not very effective anymore. We would ask the three questions to every team member, get the answers, and carry on, but we felt we were missing the grand overview.

And indeed, it often happened that stories didn't get finished. Although we knew what team members were doing, we didn't realize, as a team, that they were struggling to get things done in time.

So we changed the format of the stand-up slightly: Instead of letting each team member answer the three questions, we went over the stories on the Scrum board and the tasks that belonged to it, top to bottom. For each of these tasks, the person who worked on it told how it was progressing.

This way it was easier to spot that a story was not progressing or that the priority order wasn't honored. When all the stories were discussed, team members who didn't speak yet could speak and impediments were raised.

Note that you get clearer insight into the progress of stories this way, but that it is harder to remember who is doing what. But it is worth trying this format if asking the three questions is not giving the right results.

3.4 Stand-Ups: Getting It Right

"Hey, shouldn't we have a stand-up? Ah, you're already there. Who has the ball?"

If the team doesn't look forward to the stand-up, try to return to the basics.

- Start on time. Always.
- End on time, even if it is not finished. Cut all discussions short.

- Stick rigorously to the three questions:
  1. What did I do yesterday?
  2. What will I do today?
  3. What are my impediments?
- Introduce the talking stick.

Those simple methods can improve your stand-ups. The key to successful stand-up meetings is that you say what you have to say and listen to what all the others say. That's not different from any other meeting, but because a stand-up meeting is so short, it has to be executed with the utmost precision.

The daily stand-up meeting is a starting point for team communication, the bare minimum amount of information exchange. Use it to note what's going on, to decide on more information exchange, and to organize your work. And remember: It is never forbidden to talk *more* during the day . . .

CHAPTER 4

Everything on the Board

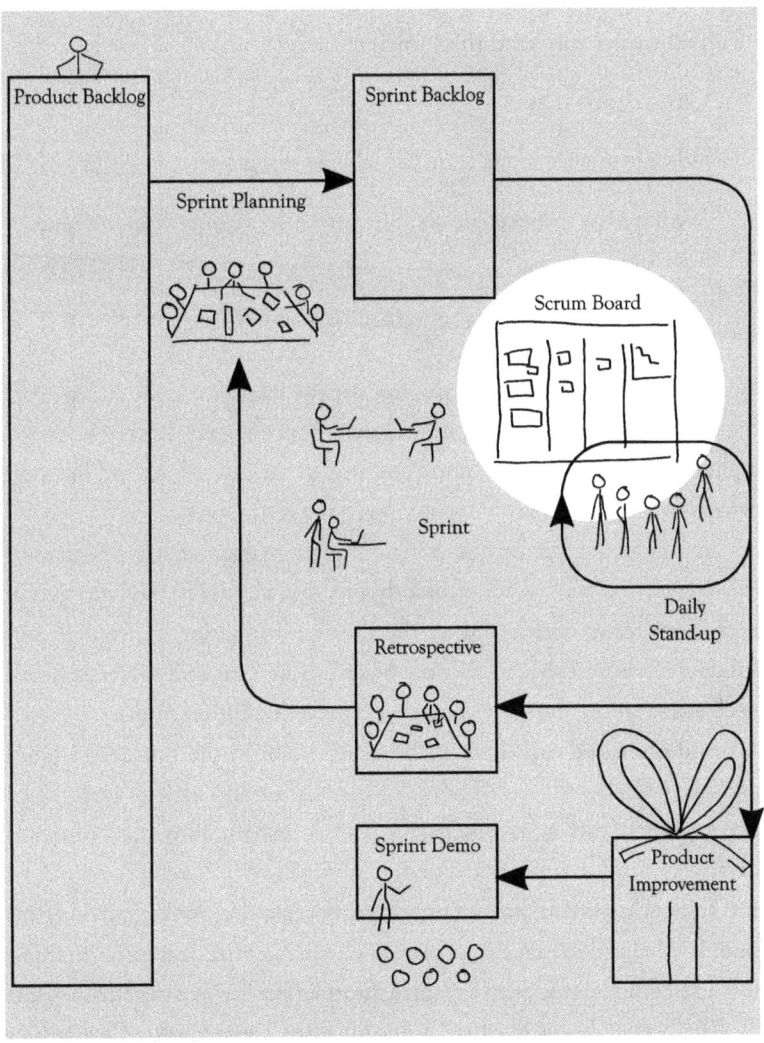

Figure 4.1 The Scrum board

"So, when does your sprint end?"

"Let me check the calendar."

"Will this story be finished this sprint?"

"I don't know; Jeff is working on that."

"Where is Chris?"

"Has anyone seen Chris today? His day off is only tomorrow, is it?"

"Did we actually send this e-mail to Gary?"

"Chris knows that . . ."

"What products is this team actually working on?"

"We have five projects, no six! But currently we only work on one. Or actually two . . ."

". . ."

When watching cop shows, you often see the inspector stand in front of a big whiteboard that shows bits and pieces from the case they're on. There's a photo of the crime scene, notes and lists in various colors, and lines and arrows to try to create some structure in the murder case.

And indeed, after a while, when three more murders have been committed and the wall is full of bloody pictures, suddenly the hero gets an idea. Something clicks, and all the messy information in front of him suddenly makes sense . . . So now he jumps in a car and drives at breakneck speed to the murderer's house, to prevent another murder.

And often the cops find in the secret room in the murderer's house another whiteboard, with photos of his victims and articles from newspapers from years ago, which give a clear insight into the murderer's deranged mind. Criminal arrested, case closed.

Those whiteboards are not only there because they look good on television. It is helpful to make information visible like that. It is easier to think, to make connections, or to organize information if you can actually see it.

The *Scrum board* is where a Scrum team keeps track of everything happening in their sprint. It helps them to organize their work and show anyone else how things are going. It is highlighted in Figure 4.1.

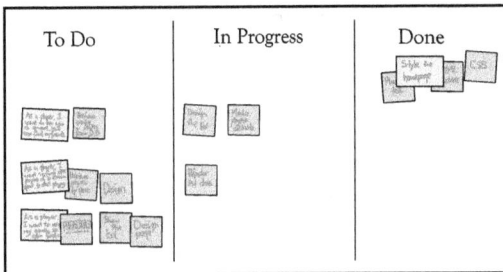

Figure 4.2 A basic Scrum board

A basic Scrum board has three columns: *To Do*, *In Progress*, and *Done* (see Figure 4.2). All the work that needs to be done is written on sticky notes and put in the first column, in priority order from top to bottom. When a team member starts to work on something, he or she puts the sticky note in the column *In Progress*, on the same height as it was in *To Do*. When the work is completed the sticky note is moved to the *Done* column.

But what you show on a Scrum board is not restricted to the work flow. It can show much more than that.

4.1 The Accessible Board

"What's the URL of the Scrum board again?"

The best Scrum boards are available all the time, by just looking up. This will make sure the information is available at all times. But it will also make it easy to keep it up to date, because if you don't, you might as well not use it.

4.1.1 Large and Near

The Scrum board should be large, close to the team, and readily available at any time. This allows everyone to look at it whenever necessary. There should be ample room around it, so that the team can gather around it at the daily stand-up; but it should also be possible to stand in front of it with a couple of team members without disturbing others. Many discussions can take place in front of the Scrum board. Make sure they can happen!

A Scrum board can be a whiteboard or just a wall. If you use a wall, it is probably better to stick a large sheet of paper on it, as it allows you to move the Scrum board if necessary. If you have your own, large team room, this may not be needed.

4.1.2 Low-Tech over Hi-Tech

Electronic Scrum boards are not very good. They are not continuously available (unless you have a very large spare screen), they don't allow you to stand in front of them and oversee all of it at once, and they miss the flexibility of the old-fashioned paper-and-pencil version.

It is easier to remember things when they are different. So handwritten notes, not exactly in a grid, with drawings and ornaments, are much easier to visualize when not in sight than square blocks on computer screens.

Scrum Board for Remote Team Members

There are various Scrum board applications that allow you to share a Scrum board over the Internet. None of them have the power and flexibility of a wall with index cards and sticky notes.

But if you are forced to use some electronic means (e.g., because you have a distributed team) you can use a physical board during the day and transfer the changes once every day to the electronic version.

Using a high-resolution webcam or publishing photographs may also work. You have to make sure that the remote team members can make their changes to the board too. They can e-mail their changes to someone near the board or use instant messaging.

If remote team members work together on another site, they can have their own Scrum board. It should be a copy of the main Scrum board; if each half of the team has a different Scrum board it may be better to split the team.

But that way, keeping the Scrum board up to date is a lot of work. If you want to avoid the extra work, get a Scrum board application, but get an extra screen in your team room that always shows the Scrum board.

4.1.3 Use Colors

Things that are different are easier to remember. In trying to make different things as different as possible, colored sticky notes and colored pens can also be very useful. Use them for tasks that are different, for stories that are not tasked yet, or for unplanned work.

4.1.4 The Board Has Two Audiences

On the Scrum board, you keep track of the progress of your work. But for whom are you doing this?

The first and most important audience is the team itself. They use the board to keep track of what they're doing: Using the familiar three columns (To Do or Stories, In Progress, and Done) they make every task and every story float from the left to the right. It is the principal tool for the team to keep track of *everything*; it's theirs and they should use it how they see fit.

But don't forget that other people may also take a look at the Scrum board once in a while: managers, to see how things are going; or stakeholders, worrying that their items are not ready in time. So be aware that you might need to answer questions about it once in a while.

It's a good idea to organize the board clearly, with the three columns on one side and a status area (with the burn-down chart, for example) on the other side. In the status area, you can also put more information for that other audience: the time of the daily stand-up, the names of the people in the team, the products the team is working on, and so on.

4.2   Everything Flows

After the team tasked the story, they conveniently put names on most of the tasks. Tim got all the tests, Jeff, as a MySQL guru, was assigned the creation of databases and tables, and Chris, who did a similar story before, was going to implement the business logic.

The sprint progressed nicely. But near the end, it became clear the story was not going to be finished. Because the team had been waiting for the database to be ready, they started late on the other tasks. Tim really didn't have time, but nobody picked up the task that had his name on it. And now Chris called in sick . . .

One reason why a sprint can fail is when tasks or stories get stuck. The board can help you in preventing that or at least in noticing it early.

4.2.1 Use Names on Tasks

Never assign tasks. The team should have the freedom at any time to decide what to do, who does it, and works together with who. If tasks are assigned to people, the flexibility of the team is killed; you create a critical path where there wasn't one.

It might come as a surprise when a certain member of the team picks up a certain task, but this is a good thing. People learn a lot when they get out of their comfort zone. The knowledge about a certain type of task is spread more evenly over the team. And the person who always did this kind of tasks is now free to do something else.

Whenever you take a task in progress, mark it with your name or initials. That makes it clear you took the responsibility to finish the task. Alternatively, create a marker (a colored sticky note or a magnet) for each team member. This has the added advantage that it becomes difficult to work on more than one task at the same time. Now everybody can see at any time who is working on what. This will make it much easier to offer help or discuss impediments.

4.2.2 Use Dots for Days Spent on Tasks

If you think that some tasks are stuck in "In Progress" for a long time, you can put a mark on each task in the "In Progress" column at the end of the stand-up meeting. Tasks that are in progress for a long time will accumulate a lot of dots. It will be a sign that something needs to happen; you can discuss it in the stand-up.

4.3   Shortest Path from To Do to Done

"Why is that story still not done?"

"Because Jennifer still needs to review my code. Look, the task is there, in To Review."

". . ."

"There, below all the others!"

Some Scrum teams use four or five columns on the board. Apart from "To Do" and "In Progress" they have "To Test" or "To Review" before "Done," or even other columns.

4.3.1 Don't Use Extra Columns

The idea of the "To Review" is that developers review the code written by other developers. The idea of "To Test" is that every task passes through the "To Test" column before it is done. The problem with extra columns is that they don't necessarily apply to every task that is on the board. How do you test an e-mail that is written? How do you review a deployment that was done?

When some tasks skip over those columns and some don't, it is actually less clear what needs to be done. There is another way to do this: Use only three columns and write extra tasks for every test or every review that needs to be done. This can just be added to the story in the "To Do" column and moves through "In Progress" and "Done" just like any other task. Every activity will be in progress at one time and done at another, so that always works.

All extra columns also have the disadvantage that the ownership of a task changes when the task goes from one column to the next. If Jeff completed code and puts it in "To Review," Laura will need to pick it up. If Jennifer finished a feature and moved it to "To Test," Tim will need to test it. Those tasks are more likely to remain orphaned than the tasks in the "To Do" column. When there is an explicit task for everything, it is much clearer who took responsibility for it.

4.4   But There Is More to Remember

The Team had a retrospective meeting, and they were discussing why they finished only two stories.

"So why didn't we finish that reporting functionality again?"

"Well, we were waiting for the template, but in the meantime, we had the production issue, you remember?"

"Yes, and don't forget that Laura was busy for a week to fix that bug we discovered last sprint. That wasn't planned, but we had to do that first."

"But actually I forgot to send that mail to ask for the template . . ."

The Scrum board is not only there for stories and tasks; it makes everything visible that is important for the sprint. If things change, it is reflected on the board.

If you put *everything* you want to keep track of on the board, there are no surprises. You get much more insight into how the sprint is going than by just looking at the burn-down chart (which doesn't tell you why) or by just attending the stand-up meetings (which only talk about today and yesterday.)

4.4.1 Unplanned Work

Whenever some unplanned work comes up, you should make a sticky note for it and put it on the board. The Scrum board is not only there to show what the status of all the work is. It also works the other way around: At any time, you can see what the status of all the team members is. That doesn't work anymore when people are working on tasks that are not on the board. It might lead the team into thinking that Jeff is doing this, while in reality he is working on that; and then the work is not done until it is too late.

You can make a special section for unplanned work on the board. This is especially useful for work that is not related to any story already on the board. This is assuming that the unplanned work is more important than all the other work in the current sprint. It should be; if not, it should wait until the next sprint.

Never take in unplanned work without considering carefully whether it is urgent enough. It is disrupting your sprint and endangering the work you committed to. Try to limit the amount of unplanned work as much as possible, postponing until next sprint what you can.

4.4.2 Impediments

If any impediments come up during the stand-up (or at any other time), it is probably a good thing to keep a list of them on the board. That way the whole team can track if they are cleared, and the Scrum Master can go over them in the daily stand-up.

If the Scrum Master is swamped with impediments, the rest of the team might offer help. After all, if every member of the team is blocked, the team cannot work anyway; it's better to help clearing the impediments early, to prevent this from happening. A clear (and visible) list of impediments helps noticing this in time.

4.4.3 Next

Sometimes you realize some work needs to be done while you are working on something else. A "Next" corner on the board can be used to hold these. The Product Owner should pick them up and work them into the product backlog as soon as possible, but in the meantime they are at least not forgotten. And if there is a little time left in the sprint, and the Product Owner agrees, you can pick them up right away.

4.4.4 Issues

In a stand-up, you shouldn't discuss things for too long; you should decide to discuss things outside the meeting. If there are a lot of things to discuss, you can make a list of them in the "Issues" corner. Also things that need to be discussed later (when the release is done or when the Product Owner is back from holiday) can be parked there.

4.4.5 Improvement Items

If you came up with some good resolutions in the retrospective meeting, it might be a good idea to have them on the board as well. This way the team will read them at least once every day (at the stand-up.)

It will also be easier for anyone in the team to bring it up if needed: "Hey, according to our improvement items there we check in working code daily. Are we still doing that?"

Don't forget to remove them after the next retrospective, and replace them with new ones. If you don't touch the sticky notes with improvement items for a long time, you will no longer see them and then they don't help anymore.

Holidays, Reminders, Cartoons

There are more things that can be useful to keep on the board, although by now you might need a second board:

- Especially in the holiday season: Who is gone from when to when?
- "Team event 12 March!"
- "Source code repository not available from Friday 17:00 to Monday 8:00 because of maintenance"
- Last week's XKCD

4.5   The Scrum Board: Getting It Right

"So, when does your sprint end?"

"Will this story be finished this sprint?"

"Where is Chris?"

"Did we actually send this e-mail to Gary?"

"What products is this team actually working on?"

". . ."

"Look at the board!"

Figure 4.3 The Scrum board in real life

The Scrum board is your one-stop source of information about the progress and state of the sprint. Anything that has to do with the working process can be stored there. This is not design, documentation, and code; they go somewhere else.

Try to put everything that is relevant on the board. If the board is used for everything, you never have to guess where to look. If you can't find some information you expected on the board, put it there. Others might be looking for it as well. Take a look at Figure 4.3 to see how much can go onto a board.

Organize the board clearly. Create sections on it for:

- "To Do," "In Progress," "Done"
- Impediments
- Burn-down chart
- Unplanned items
- Issues
- Next
- Team members and holidays
- Improvements items
- . . . and anything else

Empty sections will invite the team to fill them. Just by creating them, you will improve the completeness of the information on the board.

Keep the Scrum board rigorously up to date. Wrong information is even worse than no information. Make the information clear, well written, and well organized. You will look at it often; make it a pleasure to look at.

Most of the Scrum board can be wiped entirely after each sprint. Only unfinished stories are carried over from one sprint to the other, but they are taken off the board, resized, reprioritized, and put on the board again. What is left from the last sprint is the velocity. And lots of working software.

CHAPTER 5

Planning Is Half the Work

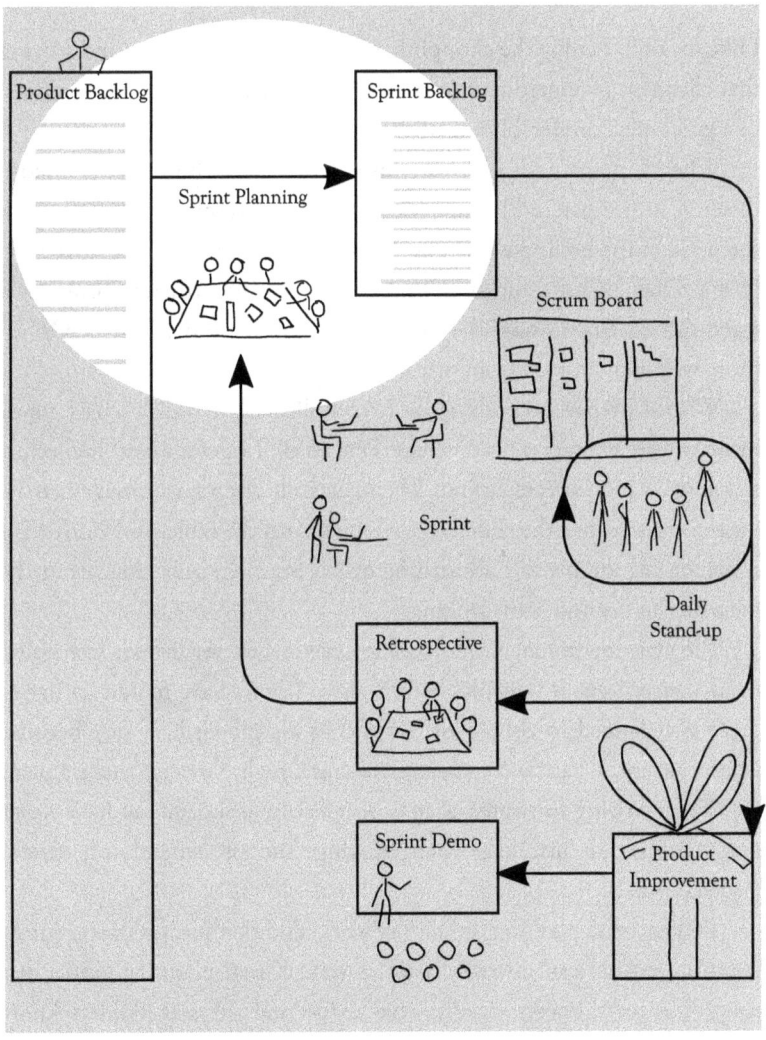

Figure 5.1 The sprint planning

The Team is doing a planning meeting. Gary, the Product Owner, brought along some documents, specifications and printed e-mails, and The Team tries to understand what they mean. After they have organized it into a prioritized backlog, they want to size the items to find out how many of them they can take into the sprint. But then Gary tells The Team they really have to do all of them. After all, the product is due next month, and they are already behind schedule . . .

I like to cook. I enjoy the chopping, mincing, frying, boiling, and stirring that changes raw ingredients into something better. And I like the reward of a good meal, preferably together with family and friends.

When I prepare an everyday dish, I just start chopping an onion, throw it in the pan, add some vegetables and seasoning, and then cook the pasta in the boiling water that I didn't forget to put on the stove first. It is a rather organic and messy process, which nevertheless results in a tasty dish usually. I know the things to do and the order in which to do them well enough that I can just start.

When I prepare something more complicated, or a dish I have never made before, the process is different. First of all, I carefully read the recipe, to know what is expected of me. Then I actually chop the onions, slice the vegetables, and put the different ingredients on the table, so I don't have to search for them while something else is burning; only then I put the pans on the fire and start cooking.

The preparation makes the cooking easier; whenever there is something needed *right now*, it is available right now; I don't have to add an ingredient that I need to chop first, or find in a cupboard, or buy because I don't have it. Chances for success are much higher when I make a plan.

When writing software, often a new feature is a dish you have never made before. So just like when cooking, success depends on careful preparation.

They say that planning is half the work, and that means a good sprint planning session can save you a lot of time. Good planning works two ways: The team knows exactly what to do and the stakeholders know exactly what you are doing. Those two ways help each other. If the team knows what to do, they deliver lots of working software; if the stakeholders know what is in the works and when it is due, they are more likely to leave the team working on it and not interfere.

Effective sprint planning consists of three components: accurate sizing, careful tasking, and full commitment. If you get those three right, you can work effectively and undisturbed for a full sprint afterward. See the planning in Figure 5.1.

But it is still not easy to get it right. How do you size well? How do you get the most out of tasking? And how can the team confidently commit to the sprint backlog?

5.1   Planning the Planning

"Ladies and gentlemen, this is the planning meeting, isn't it? So this sprint you need to do the web interface; the specifications will come tomorrow, and the design is created as we speak. You can keep yourselves busy in the meantime, I trust. You've seen the web site's mock-up in my presentation, haven't you? Is there anything else you need? So, let's go!"

If planning is half the work, then preparing the planning is vital. For the team to be able to do an effective planning session, not only must the session be prepared, but enough of the product backlog must be in good shape as well, or else there is no work to do.

5.1.1 Preparing the Session

For a good sprint planning, the team must be able to work uninterrupted for a couple of hours. So make sure you have a dedicated room or area, with no distractions.

What do you need to bring to a planning session?

- The user stories, written or printed on cards, large enough that you can read them from a distance
- Spare paper, to write new stories if necessary
- Sticky notes, pens, markers
- A whiteboard might come in handy

- Any information that might help in understanding the stories, for reference
- Lots of coffee, tea, or other refreshments

One more thing: The team should know the velocity from the previous sprint(s). If they don't know it by heart or it is not very well established yet, bring historical data about the previous sprints' velocity.

5.1.2 User Stories

User stories are descriptions of new features in one or two sentences of plain language. Even if your organization uses a different way of specifying requirements, it's a good idea to write user stories for use on the Scrum board. They are an easy-to-remember, short description of the work to be done.

Often, user stories are written like this:

As a system administrator, I want an easy way to deploy the server application so that I make fewer mistakes.

As a word processor user, I want errors in my Latin grammar be highlighted so that I am able to find and fix mistakes as early as possible.

Although this format is sometimes awkward, it describes features from the viewpoint of a user of your software and explicitly states the benefit for this user. There are two reasons for doing this. You will remember *why* you are implementing a feature; that will help you make decisions about design or implementation. For example, the system administrator above wants to make fewer mistakes, so "easy" really means "less error prone."

Also, sometimes you find a different way to get the same benefit to the user (e.g., instead of highlighting errors, fixing the Latin grammar mistakes right away!). If your feature description just reads "Highlight grammar errors" you might miss this opportunity.

Correctly written user stories describe tangible, finished features that can be demonstrated easily. It helps to stick to the form:

As a *<somebody>*, I want *<something>*, so that I *<benefit>*.

Usually, if it is hard to put in this format, it is hard to demo as well. Take the following example:

> As a user, I want an expert system of Latin grammar rules to be stored in a database.

"As a user" was just put in front here to adhere to the format. As a user I don't care what an expert system is, let alone where it is stored. As a user, I want to write correct Latin. This last user story is not complete (it describes no benefit to the user) and describes an implementation, not a feature.

It will show when you try to demo this feature. Highlighted grammar errors are much easier to demonstrate than database contents.

5.1.3 Ready (or READY)

Before you can do a planning, the backlog must be ready. And that means that there are enough stories to keep the team busy for a sprint, that every story is well enough understood that they can start working on it, and that the priority order of the stories is clear. The Product Owner is responsible for getting the backlog ready. He or she usually doesn't do this all alone, but the Product Owner has to make sure it is done when the sprint begins.

During the sprint planning, the Product Owner should be present to reprioritize stories, take them out of the backlog, or change them, if there is a need for that. For example, if a story turns out to be much more difficult than the Product Owner expected, he or she can reconsider whether it needs to be done at all. Or if a feature is not necessary as the team explains there is already another way to do it, the story may change ("improve the documentation" instead of "implement new feature"). Of course, if the backlog is really ready, this will not happen very often.

The team should never start working on stories that are not really ready. If requirements are unclear or, for example, translations are not available, or there are no machines to install on, the team cannot work efficiently on that story. They should give it back to the Product Owner and advise to postpone it to a later sprint.

READY Instead of Just Ready

Jeff Sutherland, coinventor of Scrum, uses a more formal notion of "READY." He states that READY is for the Product Owner as what DONE is for the team. Stories should never leave the Product Owner's hands before they are READY, and the Definition of READY is an important concept for the Scrum team to succeed.

5.2   Size Matters

The Team is doing a planning meeting.

"Well, the last four stories on the sprint backlog were not really finished, so we continue working on them. Then I guess I should also do this one, and of course Jeff does the database story. So . . ."

"Guys! Guys!", the Product Owner said.

"Yes?"

"Do you have any idea when this will be finished? Do you have any idea when *anything* on the product backlog will be finished?"

Although sizing is a bit of a black art, it is an important planning tool. Not only is it necessary for the team to take the guesswork out of the sprint planning, but for the longer term, your stakeholders need a longer-term plan.

Planning in Scrum revolves around one concept: velocity. That is all you need to plan the future.

5.2.1 Establish the Team's Velocity

The purpose of a planning meeting is to come up with a sprint backlog: exactly enough work to keep the team busy for one sprint. How do you know what is enough work? The key to that is the team's *velocity*. The velocity of the team is the amount of work they can do per sprint.

For this, you need to establish a size for each of your stories, because not every story has the same complexity or will take the same time to implement. The sizes don't have to be absolute though: You don't have to estimate the duration of the stories' implementation in hours or days.

Doing that is hard anyway. Most human beings are overly optimistic. They forget the time it takes to set up their systems, remember what they were doing yesterday, drink coffee, and numerous other things you do besides the actual work. The error made is more or less systematic: Estimates are a factor off, but always the same factor off.

Using velocity solves this by actually measuring how long it takes to do the work after you have sized it, thus establishing that factor. Instead of guessing how much you're off and compensating for it, you just measure how much you're off and use that factor on your future sizes.

So for your first sprint, you estimate the size of a number of stories on the top of your product backlog, and take in to the sprint as much as you think you can handle. For the next sprint, you know how much you did in the previous sprint, and use that number to guide you. Over time, your velocity will become established, as you can look at the average velocity (and the trend) over the past few sprints.

5.2.2 Use Story Points Instead of Days

When you use velocity to measure how much work you can do, you don't need to estimate in person-days or person-hours anymore; they don't directly match with real days or hours anyway. Instead, you can start using *story points*.

A story point is a unit of measure that is made up by the team itself. You just take a medium-sized story and assign it a size, and then you size all other stories in comparison to that one. A story point thus has only meaning within the team; another team may have completely different story points.

At first sight, story points might look less precise than person-days, but they are not. After all, it is the same experts estimating the relative complexity of the same work to be done; only the unit of measure differs. But if you size in ideal days, you are suggesting to the stakeholders (and maybe even yourselves) that you talk about real time. The arbitrary story points don't suggest that.

Using story points also invites the team not to think in too much detail. Instead of trying to imagine all the days of work you need to do on a story, you compare it to similar stories. That is easier to do and you're less likely to miss chunks of work. Also, it is less determined individually. An expert in the field might estimate many days less than a novice, even though they might consider the size the same.

5.2.3 Let's Look at a Detailed Example

Let's look at an example project. The team is working on an online web-based board game server. On the website, you can find a collection of turn-based board games, like chess, checkers, and maybe card games as well, like bridge or poker. There is a lobby where you can find other players for games, and maybe you can form subcommunities or groups of people who like certain games and often play together.

A user story for this system could be:

As a player, I want to find other players of a certain game, so that we can start playing.

Another one could read:

As a player, I want to see who is online, so I can find my friends.

Now let's look at the last user story. Without going into too much detail, the team can establish that this requires a lookup in the table of players currently logged in. It requires designing a page where the players are shown. And probably you need to be able to click on a name to see the details about a player.

The screen with the player details is a different story, with its own size; maybe we implement that first. For this story, we just need to make sure something happens if you click on a player. Given that scope, let's compare to the first story. This would require a lookup in the table of players currently logged in, combined with their game interests. They need to be shown on a screen as well and be clickable, very similar to the other user story.

So it is safe to say that these two stories are similar in size. They might not take exactly the same amount of hours to implement, but the difference will not be large. Let's just assume them equally sized from now on.

Another one:

As a player, I want register the board games I play, so other players can find me.

This is where a player can register their interests. It requires a screen where you can see the supported games, which is a list that needs to be looked up. It requires storing those preferences as well. And to get it right, you should also be able to change your preferences, removing a game from the list if you're no longer interested.

Maybe this story is a bit larger than the previous two. The team could decide that it is one-and-a-half times as large, or two times. But note that it is not necessary to go into much detail on how to do table lookups or what the screen looks like exactly: It is enough to realize that other stories contain the same bits and that it will be a similar amount of work to implement those bits.

5.2.4 Use a Burn-Down Chart

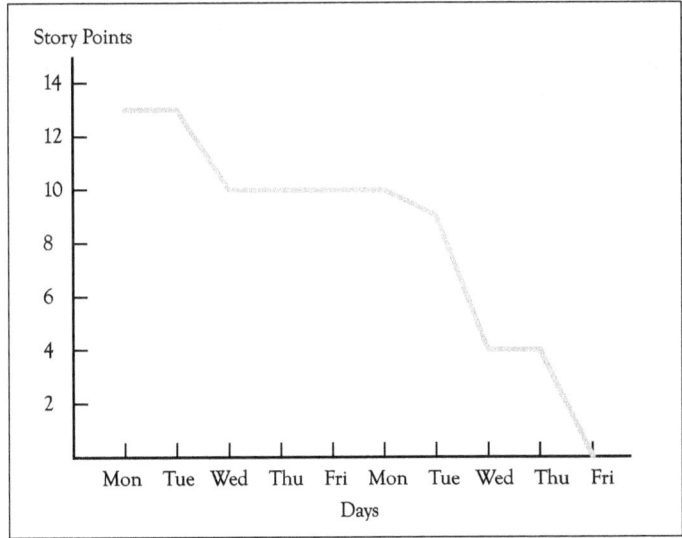

Figure 5.2 A burn-down chart

If you have sized the work of the team for the sprint, you can create a *burn-down chart*. A burn-down chart is a simple graph where the amount of work that is still to be done is on the vertical axis and the days in the sprint are on the horizontal axis. An example of a burn-down chart is shown in Figure 5.2.

Every day in the sprint, you add up the amount of work that still needs to be done. If all goes well, the line goes down and ends at the bottom at the end of the sprint. If the line stays horizontal for too long, you might not finish the sprint; if the team burns down story points too fast, you might need to add some work to the sprint.

5.2.5 What's the Use of Velocity for the Team?

For the team, it is important to know their velocity as well. First of all, the team can use it to forecast how many stories they can take into the sprint. This will add some confidence to the planning.

Another reason to keep an eye on your velocity is to see if it improves. If impediments are cleared, if the team is working together for longer, and if the knowledge increases and collaboration between team members improves, your velocity will go up. This is of course a good thing: The team becomes more productive.

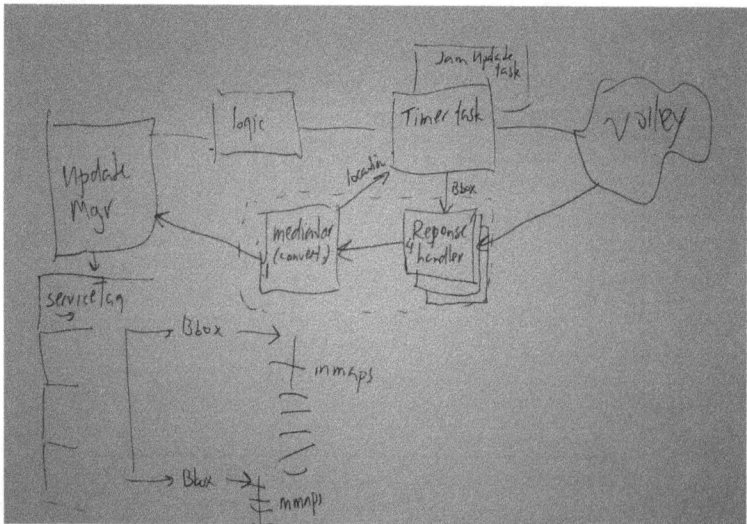

Figure 5.3 A photograph of an architecture diagram to be e-mailed

However, your velocity can also go down. That needs some investigation. Why did it go down? Is it just because team members were on holiday or did you do less work per available person-day? Are there external circumstances that explain it? This could be a good starting point for discussion in the retrospective meeting.

Meeting by Phone

During planning and sizing, it is vital that all team members have access to enough information about the user stories to size and task them. Whether it is one of the team members explaining things or information being e-mailed around before the meeting doesn't matter, as long as everyone has it.

If part of the team is off-site, make sure before the planning meeting that they have a list of all the stories and other available information. If they don't, half of the meeting will be about pointing the remote team members to the right information.

Sometimes a lot of designing is going on during the tasking, including drawing diagrams on whiteboards. These can be hard to communicate in words. A camera and e-mail might help here: Make a picture of the whiteboard and send it to the remote team members or use a webcam. See Figure 5.3 for an example of such a picture.

So make sure you have a computer with a network connection on both sides if you are meeting by phone. That way you can quickly exchange information without interrupting the conversation too much.

5.2.6 Size before the Planning Meeting

The product backlog is truly "ready" if enough items in it are sized *before* the sprint planning. That way, the team knows exactly how many stories they can take into the next sprint; they just peel stories off the top of the prioritized product backlog until the total equals their velocity for the next sprint (or a bit less or a bit more). The Product Owner can then choose to change the order a little to cram in more short stories or take out short stories in favor of a long one.

In reality, you usually have to do a bit more in the planning meeting. Some stories from the previous sprint might still be unfinished and need to be looked at again. Some new stories might have been created recently and need to be done in this sprint. But it is good to make sure your product backlog is always as ready as possible.

If all sizing is done in the sprint planning meeting, it will take a large part of the time. Maybe some team members see the stories for the first time and need to get their head around it. But after that, the Product Owner probably will have to reorder, run around and talk to people, and tell lots of people bad news, because the actual contents of the sprint come more or less as a surprise. In the meantime, the team is waiting.

If the sizing is done well ahead, only the last few stories are uncertain, but even that is known in advance. That means the Product Owner can decide on the spot what goes in and what not.

It is of course possible to size stories for the *next* sprint in the sprint planning meeting. But it is better to have separate sizing meetings or to size one or two items every day. You could, for example, do that right after the stand-up meeting, when the whole team and the Product Owner are present anyway.

5.3   Sizing Is Not Easy

That was a painful planning meeting. The product backlog was huge, and the Product Owner seemed determined to cram in as much as possible. "We have to finish on time, else we cannot ship before Christmas."

To make matters worse, the CTO attended the meeting and helped determining sizes. And even though The Team objected and argued and haggled, he had the final word on some stories that really "shouldn't be that difficult."

Now the sprint began. Soon The Team realized it was not going to be hard to prove the CTO wrong . . .

If your sizes are wrong, your planning is not worth much. Your sizing needs to be as accurate as possible. But also the whole team must believe in them, because you cannot commit to a sprint backlog if you think it can't be done.

5.3.1 Size with the Whole Team

How do you size stories? One thing is really important: Size them with the whole team. Even if there are specialists in the team that are much better at doowopping or fiddlydiddling than others, you shouldn't let them do the sizing and ignore the other team members. There are a number of reasons for this.

If the expert sizes, the expert must do the work, or the size is not accurate. That is not a good thing in a team. It prevents working together and makes the team feel less responsible for the work.

If the expert is ill, he cannot do the work. If the team collaborated in sizing the story, they know at least what it is about and someone might be able to take over.

One person might misunderstand the story. If the whole team participates in the sizing and they heavily disagree about the size, maybe some members don't really understand the story. Then the Product Owner can explain the story better.

And last but not least, if the whole team participated in the sizing of a story and reached consensus, they will believe it can be done in that time. On the contrary, if some team members don't think a size is accurate, they will not feel very motivated to get it done in time.

5.3.2 Planning Poker

Planning Poker is a fun way to size stories that makes collaborating on sizing very easy. Using cards, each team member votes for a size, by showing a size at the count of three. If the sizes vary a lot, the high and low voters explain their size. Then you repeat voting (and discussing) until everyone agrees. Don't take the average without discussing; the whole team should participate and the whole team should agree. Don't let the discussion go on endlessly either; settle for a number if everyone can live with it.

The cards you have for voting are usually marked with Fibonacci numbers: 1, 2, 3, 5, 8, 13, and 21. The reason for the missing intermediates is that you don't get too much false precision that way. It is impossible to size as precisely as "this is 15, not 14." It is better to be forced to choose between 8 and 13 or 13 and 21.

There is a lot of information about Planning Poker available on the Internet. You can also buy professional, durable poker cards online.

5.3.3 Resize Unfinished Work

Sometimes a story from the previous sprint is not finished. Although it is very tempting to count part of its size into the sprint's velocity, it is better not to do that. After all, the story is not finished. It's hard to tell how much is, and not counting it at all will be an extra incentive to finish all stories in the next sprint.

Another thing that might appeal is to take the full 13 story points story into the next sprint and finish it within a day. Now that will look good on your burn-down chart! Again, it's better not to do that. Although the *average* velocity over several sprints will seem more accurate this way, the actual value will jump up and down very much. This will make it more difficult for the team to decide what is a good amount of story points in a sprint and might cause some unnecessary discussion and worries in the retrospective meeting.

The best way is to resize the remainder of the story. Then the size of the story as it gets into the sprint matches the work that needs to be done; it will make your velocity more stable. Also, it will make the forecasting more dependable: All work that still needs to be done is accounted for. And if the team gets better at finishing all stories, you will actually see your velocity improve, because no half-finished stories disappear between sprints.

In other words: Your velocity is not the amount of work you can do in a sprint; it is the amount of work you can *promise at the planning* and do in a sprint. If you can do more work in some sprints, that is not relevant to your stakeholders. All they are interested in is what you can deliver with confidence. Keep thinking of velocity as promised work, and make it as stable as possible. Delivering what you promise will build trust in the team.

5.3.4 Break It Down!

"Jeff, what did you do yesterday?"

"I'm still working on that story."

"And what will you do today?"

"I will continue working on it."

"Can anybody help you, maybe?"

"I don't know . . ."

If a story is a mystery to all team members except one, working together is hard. Part of planning your sprint therefore is breaking down the stories into tasks. Breaking down a story is useful for a lot of reasons:

- As a team, you will fill in the details of the story, learning what needs to be done to implement it.
- You can verify whether the size of the story still makes sense.
- As a team, you get on the same page what's in the story and what is not.
- If the tasks are independent enough, people can work on the tasks in parallel.

5.3.5 Task Your Stories

For each story, the team decides what tasks need to be done to implement it. Tasks should be relatively small (not more than one or two person-days) and written out clearly. Try to make tasks independent, so that people can work on them in parallel. Write the tasks on yellow sticky notes and stick them to the story. If anything about a story is still unclear, it will become apparent during the tasking. The Product Owner should be available to explain it again.

Typical tasks for a story look like this:

- Create a database table for the games players.
- Write a Data Access Object class for that database table.
- Implement the query to retrieve all players currently online.
- Create the screen that shows the players currently online.
- Make the player names clickable and pop-up the player details screen.

Note that these tasks are more or less independent, that the code written can be unit tested, and that they will probably take no more than a day or so. If a task is much bigger than that, break them down into more pieces.

Use your tasks also as reminders for edge cases that need to be checked, e-mails that need to be sent, or questions that need to be asked. Be as clear and complete as possible. You might not start working on this story right away, so don't assume you will remember everything.

When tasking, you are actually drafting the technical design for your implementation. It is important to do it carefully. If a story is not tasked very well, the team members that will work on it will get stuck. Investing some time now will save you a lot of time later.

Tasking is very demanding and time consuming. Make sure the team is prepared for that. Take breaks, and make sure you don't rush it.

5.3.6 Estimating Tasks

If you want to, you can make a time estimate for each task. The estimate for a task should be somewhere between half a day and 3 days; else your tasks are too small or too large. Although it means more work, estimating tasks has some advantages.

Why Don't We Estimate Tasks in Story Points?

Earlier we learned it was better to use story points, and not days, for sizing stories. So why are we estimating tasks in days?

A sprint only lasts a couple of weeks, so during tasking we go into much more detail than during sizing. For the sprint plan, it is useful to get an idea of the real amount of time each individual task will take; with that estimate, you can predict (with a certain margin) that this task will be done at that day.

With story sizing, it is different. The sizing is much more course-grained, since you only need a relative size compared to other stories. As we saw earlier, this is enough to predict what fits in a sprint or some sprints to come.

First of all, it will give you some idea what can be done when. If a task depends on another task, it is useful to know when that first task can be done. Estimating your tasks gives you the information to make a rough plan for the coming sprint.

Furthermore, you can track the duration of tasks during the sprint. If a task was estimated to take half a day but is on the "In Progress" column for 2 days, something is wrong. This can be a sign of an impediment or an early warning that a story was underestimated by the team. But maybe the person working on the task abandoned it and is working on something else. In any case, if you notice this, you can do something about it.

The added time of all tasks is also a sanity check of your story's size. If a story sized at 8 story points has 10 days of tasks on it, a 5-point story should have about 6 days. If it has only 2, you should consider resizing the story or rethink your tasks. If it has 7, it is probably OK.

You don't have to estimate tasks. If your tasks are small and well understood by the whole team, it might not be necessary to stick a time estimate to them. If tasks have very different sizes though, it is probably worth doing it. A big task that is a mystery to some team members can add a lot of uncertainty to your sprint.

5.4   Team Commitment

At the end of the planning meeting, the team should explicitly commit to the sprint backlog. They should, as a team, agree to do all the work in the coming sprint. If anyone in the team has any doubts, discuss it. Should you take in fewer stories? Should you take out that story until that investigation has been done? Should you postpone that story until Tim is back from holiday? Together with the Product Owner, the team should arrive at a sprint backlog they really feel they can complete.

Note that you can commit to a backlog without tasking it; tasking can be done during the sprint. There is a risk involved though: Sometimes you don't realize until tasking that you underestimated a story wildly. In the sprint planning, you can immediately adjust the sprint backlog with the Product Owner. If you find out halfway through the sprint, it will be an unpleasant surprise to your stakeholders. But if the team is experienced and knows the backlog well, they can consider committing without tasking. And if you manage to finish the sprint, you know you have arrived.

The team should decide what they can do in the sprint, not the Product Owner or a stakeholder or manager. If somebody pushes more work upon the team than they believe they can handle, it is not likely that they will finish it all.

The team's commitment should not be used to punish them if they don't deliver what they have promised. The only thing that you achieve if you do that is that the team will undercommit the next time. The team commitment is rather a commitment to *each other* to finish all the work.

If the team committed to the work, they will probably finish it; and if they finish the work they promised, they will make their stakeholders happy. In the end, that is going to help the team a lot as well. Happy stakeholders are much less likely to interrupt; they are more likely to wait with new work to the next sprint, especially if you tell them that this is exactly the secret of delivering on time.

5.5   Planning: Getting It Right

The Team was doing a planning meeting. After re-sizing the remaining story from the last sprint, they briefly discussed the top stories on the product backlog and decided to take the top five into the next sprint. Then Laura noted that they could take in the seventh story as well, because it was only two story points.

Sam, the Scrum Master, asked whether The Team could commit to this sprint backlog, and they all agreed it was doable.

Sam knew that the Product Owner was under pressure from the stakeholders to deliver by September. He asked: "Gary, as a Product Owner, can you live with that?"

"Of course. I'll see if we can postpone the beta by one sprint, but if not, we can probably take out the auto-complete feature and still finish on time."

Any business relies on good planning. In Scrum, a good plan depends on accurate sizing, careful planning, and a good execution of that planning.

Take your time to get the planning right. If the planning is sloppy, the sprint is not going to be any better. You will change plans frequently, disturbing your own sprint, and creating stress and uncertainty for the team and the stakeholders. And in the end, your velocity will be uncertain, making longer-term planning impossible.

But planning is not that difficult if you cut it in small pieces. Write clear stories and make sure you understand them well:

- Have them rigorously ordered by business value.
- Size them carefully with the whole team.
- Take your time for tasking.
- Then, take in as much as (and not more than) you can handle in the sprint.

That's all. Now the team can work in peace. And in the long run, the Product Owner and your stakeholders will be grateful for your strict planning: They will know exactly what you can deliver, at any time.

CHAPTER 6

Practices Make Perfect

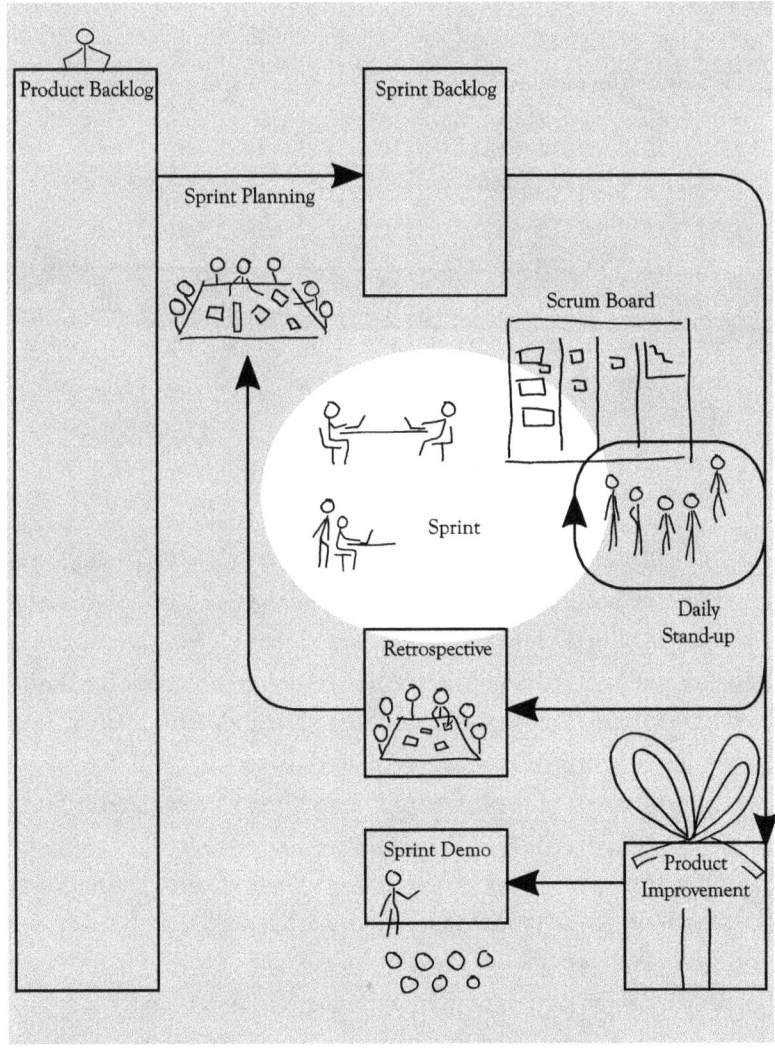

Figure 6.1 The sprint

In 2013, Robert C. Martin (better known to many as Uncle Bob) visited TomTom International BV to give a talk about development practices. An important part of his view on the difficulty of developing software is: *It is difficult to forecast the future.*

Designing software involves forecasting the future at least a little bit, because you will want to change it later. Martin explains that in the early nineties, software architects would try to come up with the perfect design that would satisfy the need of every customer forever. But the designs that came out of this were so big and complicated that it was impossible to make them or maintain them.

In 2000, the term *agile* was coined by Martin and others, to describe a different way of working. Martin describes it as follows:

> Imagine a squad of soldiers pinned down by enemy fire. Bullets are whizzing overhead. You have enough soldiers to kill the enemy; but you don't know where the enemy is. If you all stand up and fire randomly they'll cut you down. If you could point all your weapons in the right direction you could kill the enemy. So, you, as the sergeant, make an executive decision. You say: "Johnson, stand up." And now you know the direction that the bullets are coming from and you concentrate your fire, and we're sorry about Johnson.

The agile way of working is to take this first bullet: Write your code as simple as possible and release it. When the customer wants some changes, you can see how you can put abstractions in your code to make it better and easier to maintain. Instead of trying to forecast the future, you let it happen and adapt your code once you know how to do it. Then again, you release it, and when necessary, change it, until you end up with a software design that fits the features implemented and is pretty robust.

Of course you can think of some abstractions in advance, and anticipate a few changes. But otherwise, keep your design as simple as possible, or your structure will be too difficult to maintain.

Uncle Bob advises us to keep our designs as simple and flat as possible, so that we don't need to forecast the future (see Figure 6.1). But if we don't forecast the future, how can we give some structure to a large software application? How can we make sure we don't end up with a messy code base that is difficult to maintain?

6.1   Programming for Change

The Team had a big discussion about how to implement a feature.

"Really, the safest way to add the promotion pop-ups is to add the code to the footers. Then they will always show up!"

"But they don't belong there! One day, someone will see it and decide that it is a bug, and then everything breaks!"

"But if we want to do this properly, we need to rewrite the core of the responsive layout, and I don't dare to touch that code . . ."

Changing code is hard. Sometimes a body of code feels like a house of cards: If you try to change a little piece in one place, everything falls apart. Fixing bugs can feel like a game of Whac-A-Mole: Every time you fix something in one place, you caused another bug to surface somewhere else.

But writing software is all about changing existing code. Only a small percentage of a project is spent on writing completely new pieces of code. Most of the time you are changing, adjusting, and expanding existing code to add new functionality to an existing program.

So how can you make sure you can make changes without breaking old stuff? And how can you make sure your code remains maintainable, understandable, and adaptable?

6.1.1 Automated Testing

If you don't predict the future, then one thing will be certain: Things will change. Your requirements change, your software changes, and eventually, even the structure of your application or your architecture changes. This is not necessarily bad. Over time, you learn more about what you want and how you can do it, so change is inevitable, but for the better.

But you have to make sure that you don't break things while you are changing them, and to know that, you have to test. But testing software is repetitive and time consuming. The best way to make sure you carry out tests often is to automate the process.

So instead of pressing buttons, typing numbers, or manually operating software in another way, try to write programs that do that task for you. Automated tests come in many forms:

- *Unit tests*, testing a single unit of your program, like a class or a module
- *Component tests*, testing a bunch of classes or modules that together perform a certain task
- *Integration tests*, proving that components work together as intended
- *End-to-end tests*, testing the entire application

All types of tests have their strengths and weaknesses. Tests for smaller parts are easy to write and show clearly where the problem lies if the test fails, but you need a lot of them. Tests for bigger parts might show problems in your application that the more detailed tests don't reveal, because the problem lies in the interaction between parts. For a good test suite, you need tests of all kinds.

If you have a good suite of tests, you can change everything in your application with confidence. If you change something unintentionally, a test will fail, revealing that you made a mistake. The combination of tests failing will show you where to look for the defect introduced. And by fixing it immediately you make sure you don't make matters more complicated, for example, by writing code around the bug to hide it, which you might do unintentionally if a problem is hard to find.

Without automated tests, you'll need to test manually for every significant change you make to your software. Testing will become more time consuming over time, as your application grows. So your testing time will become an ever-growing part of your development.

If your automated test suite grows together with your application, you don't run into this situation. All you have to do is run the tests after every significant change, and fix the bugs that you find.

6.1.2 Test-Driven Development

Test-driven development (TDD) means you write automated tests first, then implement the code to make the tests pass. Ideally, by the time the whole system is ready, you have automated tests for every bit and piece of it.

TDD shapes your development in a good way. It encourages you to write testable code, because you think about the test before you write the code. Testable code is usually loosely coupled code, which is easier to maintain. You will also write the minimum amount of code necessary, as there is no real reason to write more code if the tests all pass.

But TDD has another advantage: Because you write your tests first, you will always have tests for all your code. If you write tests last, they are sometimes skipped because of time pressure or lack of urgency—if you write code and test it manually and everything works, you might get the feeling that everything is done. If you wrote your tests first, you actually *are* done.

If you find bugs later, you first add tests to reproduce those bugs and only then fix them. Then you run all the tests again. This will make sure that the bug is really fixed, that it will not return later, and that you didn't break anything else in the process.

TDD is a possible test strategy that may fit in well with yours. There is a lot of information about it online.

6.1.3 Continuous Integration

Continuous integration will help you in making sure that tests are running all the time and that you don't run into surprises later. The concept means that you take all the code written by all the developers regularly, integrate it, and then run all the tests to verify that everything is working correctly. Needless to say, you want to automate this process.

A *build server* helps you perform these tasks, by building and testing the software for you. Many systems exist that can do this automatically when something changes in your version control system. That way, you will be warned when anybody in your team broke anything—allowing you to fix it quickly, when the error is still easy to spot and understand.

6.1.4 *Refactoring*

Refactoring of code means changing the structure of your code, how functions, objects, and modules work together. This is sometimes necessary if a new feature cannot be easily implemented in the structure your code currently has. Indeed, if you don't create a big design up-front, you might need to change the structure of your code more often.

But if your test automation and continuous integration are in place, this is not a dangerous thing to do: Failing tests will reveal if you changed something that you didn't want to change. Refactoring is something that you should do continuously and routinely, to make the structure of your code more suitable for the new features that you want to implement.

6.1.5 *Emergent Architecture*

If you follow the best practices described here, you don't need to define a large and complicated architecture up-front. Instead, you will see your architecture develop as your application grows larger. This is what is called *Agile Architecture* or *Emergent Architecture*.

The difference with the practice of making your design up-front is that you are not trying to predict the future—at least not too much of it. Instead, you allow yourself to change your architecture without breaking features, by making sure the functionality of your code is continuously verified.

This way of working is more flexible and, in the end, much faster than trying to predict the future. Experience has shown that we are not very good at that: Predesigned architectures usually also need to be changed. If you design for change, it is much easier to pull that off, and you didn't spend time on designing up-front to begin with.

Mary Poppendieck on Construction Work

Building software used to be compared with building houses. It even borrows a lot of the terminology, like *building* and *architecture*. But as explained here, you shouldn't assume the two are too similar or blindly apply building solutions to making software.

When constructing buildings, architects actually design in much detail what the building will look like, before the construction starts. The final image of what a building will look like is much clearer than how a software product will behave.

But in an article written in 2002, Mary Poppendieck explains something about construction work that is not so well known. It is done in a way that is much more similar to the way agile teams work than you might think. In construction work, planning ahead is very difficult, as suppliers, subcontractors, and workers all have different schedules, and the design of the building is seldom final. So plans are made for days instead of weeks and adapted to reality whenever necessary, using short planning cycles that are very similar to sprints.

6.2   A Team That Works as a Team

"Can someone fix that data saving bug before the demo?"
"I don't know. Jeff wrote that code . . ."

There are a lot of reasons for team work. It supports continuity, if more than one person understands the work being done. It reduces the risk of losing knowledge, for example, if someone leaves the company. And it improves the quality if more than one pair of eyes has seen the work produced.

But working as a team asks for a certain attitude in the team members, to work in a way that supports it. You have to adapt your ways of working to the team.

6.2.1 Code Is Not Private

You do not own the code you write. Most code is read far more often than it is written, because programmers after you will need to adapt it to add new features to the software.

That means you should write for readability. That is difficult: If you are really focused on a problem, it is hard to imagine that other people don't understand what you do at that moment.

There is one way to find out: Let other people read your code and comment on it. Reading it with fresh eyes, they will come up with improvements that you never thought about. And they might even find a bug or two in the code you've just written.

6.2.2 Pair Programming Instead of Code Reviews

There are drawbacks to code reviews as well. If one person is doing all the code reviews for the team, he or she can become the "teacher" or "boss" handing out the "grades" in the eyes of the others. This is certainly not good for team spirit.

On the other hand, if everyone is taking an equal share in reviewing code, you cannot expect all reviews to be equally good. Reviewing code is hard, and for many people it is much less entertaining than writing new code, so some people will skim over the code and make some general comments instead of trying to really understand it.

Having every team member review every piece of code might be too time consuming. Reviewing with the whole team can be difficult to organize. It can be worth it for very important or very complex pieces of code, but it may be too much overhead to do it for everything.

There is also the danger of people assuming that their code doesn't have to be good because they know it will be reviewed. They can then conveniently move the blame to (or at least share it with) the reviewer.

There is an alternative: pair programming. If you program together, you are effectively reviewing each other's code continuously, back and forth. Also, you are fixing the issues you find and learning from it continuously, without putting it off till later. And since you are doing it together, you feel much less like someone is grading you. It is a lot more fun than reviewing code too.

Pair programming is intensive though. Maybe you don't want to do it all day, and at least you should take frequent breaks while doing it. Also, don't always pair up with the same person. You may develop a lack of sensitivity for each other's typical mistakes if you always work in the same pair.

6.2.3 Review for Information

Even if you have written code together, you might offer it for review to other team members. They can read the code so they know what is going on.

This is especially useful if it is an important piece of code, like a core algorithm or structure, or if the code is instructive, offering a good solution to a type of problem you might encounter again later. If you get into the habit of sharing code like that, everyone in the team will have a better understanding of how things work.

Remote Pairing

Pairing over the phone might sound impossible, but there are actually tools available that make it doable.

Many video-conferencing tools allow you to share the screen. If you both have a headset and you share the screen, you can pair program very effectively. Some tools even allow you to share control, so you can both type and operate the mouse.

If you only have a telephone available, it is more difficult to pair up. It might still be useful to work together, reading out code snippets aloud and referring to file names and line numbers.

Remote pairing is also a very effective way of making the remote worker feel part of the team. It is a good idea to let the remote workers pair as much as possible, as they are not taking part in anything else that happens in the office.

6.2.4 Shared Ownership

If you share all the code you write, have it reviewed or write it together, you will get a feeling of *shared ownership* in the team: No pieces of code will belong to a person; everyone in the team will feel responsible for every piece of code.

This is very important, for two reasons. First of all, team members will not become bottlenecks in the development of new code. If a bug is found and needs to be fixed or a new feature is developed, there is no need to wait for one owner of the code to be available or to return from holiday. And even more important: If the single owner of the code leaves the team or company, they have to do a big handover, which is a risk for your software.

But that is not the only reason. If the team shares the ownership of the software they create, they will also share the pride of their creation and the feeling of responsibility for it. They will want to make it work well, and work better, and they will never say things like: "that's not my part" or "that should be fixed by someone else." Thus shared ownership makes you a better team.

6.3   Team Organization

"Do we have that button ready?"

"Yes, everything except the art work."

"And is that code tested?"

"We'll send it off to the testers after the sprint."

"And what if they find any bugs? Or if the user experience department disagrees with the color change?"

"Then we'll fix it in the next sprint . . ."

In every software project, there are dependencies between parts: Development and graphics design depends on interaction design, testing depends on code being written, and pieces of code depend on other pieces of code.

It is not easy to oversee all those dependencies. And indeed, maybe it is better not to try to do all that in advance. If you organize your teams in the right way, you don't have to.

6.3.1 Multidisciplinary Teams

The ideal Scrum team is a multidisciplinary team: designers, developers, testers, architects, all together in a single team. If you have people in your team who can do all of the tasks, you never have to wait too long: If you need something from them, you can just ask.

And indeed this is how a good Scrum team solves their dependencies: by having short communication lines and just get things done. When the people you need are inside your team, you always have easy access to them, and you don't need a large and complicated plan to have some of their time.

6.3.2 But There Really Is Not Enough to Do!

It may not be practical to have specialists for everything in your team, as your team might become very large, and there might not be enough work for everyone. So it is better to have all team members become generalists. If multiple team members know a little bit of something, you can get things done together. If you really need a specialist, you can ask for help for a period of time. But sharing the knowledge inside your team makes sure you don't depend completely on someone outside the team.

For very specialist jobs, like graphical design, this might not work. If you don't have enough work to keep a graphical designer busy full time, maybe he or she can join the team part-time. Ideally, the graphical designer sits in your team room for the days he or she is working for you, so you have easy access for questions and feedback.

If the specialist is not part of your team, the work he or she does becomes a dependency. In that case it is best to have the work done before the sprint in which you need it; that way the team does not have to wait or hunt down the specialist during the sprint. This might slow down the work overall.

Dependencies inside the team can be solved when they occur, by talking to each other. Dependencies outside the team must be solved by careful planning. This requires that you predict which dependencies you will find and that you have the work done earlier, so all in all there is a bigger chance of planning mismatches or waiting times. If you can help it, keep the dependencies inside your team.

Waiting Is Not Very Agile

At the retrospective, a tester said that he had been waiting for most of the sprint for a developer to help him with something. This was of course caused by lack of communicating about that problem, but one developer lamented: "Waiting is not very agile."

Try to prevent waiting as much as possible. Ask questions, ask for help, try to learn how to do things yourself; and get as many trades in your team as possible, because communication and alignment inside your team is easier than outside.

6.4   Documentation

"Can anyone help me getting this application to build?"

"Wait a second, I'm searching. I had a document on my hard drive two years ago."

Many developers are not very fond of writing documentation. And in the Agile Manifesto it is stated that working software is more important than comprehensive documentation, which is certainly true. But that doesn't mean that you shouldn't write any documentation.

There are quite a few tricks to writing effective documentation. But the following things are important for effective agile documentation.

6.4.1 Keep It Small

Documentation has a tendency to rot. The code that it applies to changes, the features that are described evolve or are removed, but the documentation is not kept up to date, so after a while, the documentation doesn't match the product anymore. But bad documentation is worse than no documentation.

So it is important to keep your documentation as small as possible. Small documents are easier to read and easier to update. Resist the temptation to document everything in great detail: Keep it short and to the point.

6.4.2 Know What to Document

If the team is good at sharing knowledge and sharing responsibility for the application they write, it is not very urgent to write detailed source code documentation that describes how everything fits together: That is common knowledge within the team. It doesn't hurt to describe large design decisions, but you don't have to write in English what you have written in a programming language before.

Also, if you have the habit of refactoring code where needed, the more detail your documentation has, the faster it gets out of date. But apart from that, it is not very relevant anyway. So concentrate your effort on areas where it matters most.

Important documentation describes *how to do* things, especially if it is not very obvious. There are a lot of types of how-tos that you can write:

- How to use a piece of software
- How to accomplish a certain task using a piece of software
- How to build and run a piece of software
- How to add another screen or button or command line option to existing software
- How to decide where a new module goes
- How to extend a data structure

The good thing about this type of documentation is that it helps you to move to the future, instead of describing how things went in the past. Don't write things up for posterity; try to write for future generations instead.

6.4.3 Iterate, Iterate

Since documentation rots, you have to keep it fresh. So every time you touch a piece of code, you have to touch the documentation that goes with it, whether it is technical documentation or user documentation.

To make it easy to do so, keep the following points in mind:

- Make sure the documentation is close to the source or referred to from the source.
- Keep documentation in a centralized place, so that there is only one version of it.
- A versioning mechanism for documentation is very valuable.
- Make sure that documentation is easy to edit and doesn't require exotic tools.

Consider using a wiki for your documentation. A lot of good, free wiki software is available on the Internet. Wikis are centralized, editable from your browser, and usually have versioning built in. So a wiki fits most of the points above already. Keeping the documentation in your version control system may also work. Using locally stored Word documents will lead to problems.

6.5   Team Work: Getting It Right

"It's hard to make predictions, especially about the future."

—Niels Bohr

Making software is a dynamic process. It is not a matter of following an easy, prepared recipe; it is a long and winding road instead.

To make sure you don't get lost, you have to work together as a team. And the team can use all the help they can get. So to grow as a team, invest in the right areas:

- Get testing tools in place.
- Build a continuous integration system.
- Code together, read each other's code, share ownership.
- Keep your code alive and fresh by rigorous refactoring.
- Share and build knowledge within the team about everything you need, to reduce dependencies.
- Document just enough so you don't lose time or knowledge, and keep your documents fresh, just like your code.

If you get these right, your team will get autonomy and a sense of responsibility for the product they make. And because waiting on others is reduced to a minimum, you can truly focus on the work you do, which means you deliver quality software faster than ever before.

CHAPTER 7

Demo, Demo

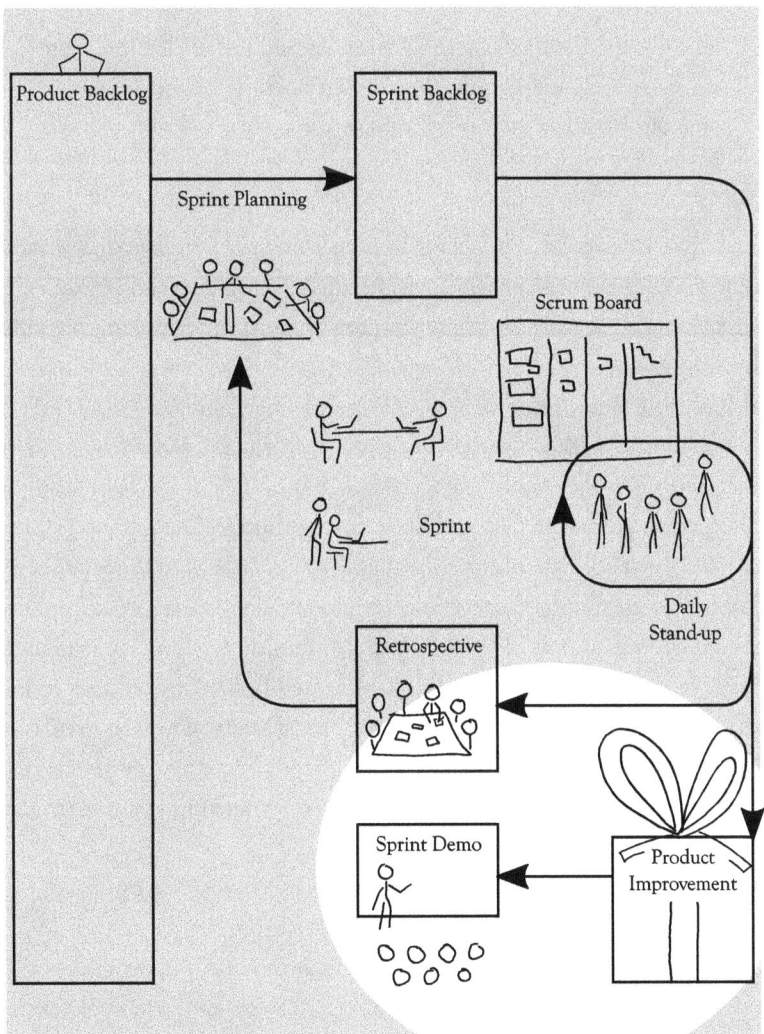

Figure 7.1 The sprint demo

The Team is ready with their sprint! Yesterday afternoon, a room was booked, a big screen was arranged for, and The Team frantically knotted the last loose ends to have a nice and shiny demo.

Not all features were demoable, of course. The sprint was not entirely finished. Some things couldn't be demoed because the parts using it weren't there yet. Some things couldn't be demoed because nothing visible had changed. But for those, some really nice PowerPoint slides were prepared.

So now the demo starts. And who's attending? Well, The Team is, of course. But despite the very compelling e-mail invitation sent out to just about everybody in the company (who matters, anyway) . . . nobody else showed up.

TomTom International BV used to be a company making general software for all types of handheld computers like Palm Pilots and Pocket PCs; we specialized in car-navigation products later. At the same time we were working on our first car-navigation application, we were also making V-Rally, the famous first-person racing game, for Palm and Pocket PC.

Of course a lot of jokes were made about making a cross between the two, where we would race on real map data. Or navigate using a first-person view, which looked like a more promising idea.

The owners of the company wouldn't even allow us to think about it. We had an important international event coming where we would present the new navigation software, and there was no time to lose and so much work to do before we were ready. Until one of our coworkers spent his weekend implementing a rough version of a 3D view, where the map was laid out in perspective on the screen and the instruction arrows were projected on it, which was surprisingly effective in making you understand what turn to take next.

He showed his experiment to Pieter Geelen, one of the owners of the company, on Monday. And despite having forbidden us to even think about this before, he said: "We've got to have this. Let's change the plan."

We changed the plan, implemented the 3D view properly, and released our car-navigation application with that feature, which set the standard for many navigation systems that came after.

What happened here shows the power of a demo. They say that seeing is believing, and that certainly goes for software. Sometimes it is difficult to believe in the value of a feature before you can actually see it working. Doing a demo gives you a great opportunity to solicit feedback from your stakeholders; don't miss that opportunity. Do a demo at the end of each sprint, as seen in Figure 7.1.

But there are more reasons why it is important to have demos. Now how can you make sure you have well-received demos that don't take forever to prepare?

7.1   Don't Move Deadlines

"The story is almost finished. Can't we demo on Friday?"

"I'd rather work on this story than waste time on a demo!"

"If we move the deadline to Monday we can have 20 story points done instead of 10."

"Who knows we have a demo today?"

Scrum is made of fixed-length sprints. If you have 3-week sprints, you have a deadline every 3 weeks. The sprint demo helps to keep the deadline fixed.

But having a demo can be difficult; it may feel like a waste of time, especially if nobody showed up last time. If not everything is finished, the demo can be embarrassing. But not having a demo is worse. Demos shape your sprint, and the shape of your sprints determines the success of your team.

Sometimes it can be very tempting to move the deadline a couple of days; it will allow you to finish a bit more and prepare a bit better. Although that might be true, it is a bad idea to move deadlines. A moving deadline tends to mover forever; if you start shifting it into the future, it will be very hard to fix it again. And then the whole idea of a clear, crisp break between this sprint and the next will be gone.

7.1.1 Deadlines Are Seldom Internal

Once you have revealed your schedule to anyone, people will start relying on it. After all, you committed to doing those stories in this sprint, so your stakeholders, business people, and managers will expect you to finish on that day. It will be much easier for them to adapt if you tell them "We did this, this and that, but we didn't start this and that," than if you tell them "We're still working on it, it should be ready any moment."

7.1.2 Velocity Needs a Timebox

There's another reason to stick to your deadlines: The team's velocity is meaningless if your sprints have different lengths. Velocity is an important planning tool. Actually it is the only statistic about productivity a Scrum team produces, but if used correctly, it is the only thing you will ever need. Provided, of course, it is accurate and stable.

A sprint demo makes a deadline much stricter, as it will be at least embarrassing not to have the demo at the set date. So book your demo meeting at the beginning of the sprint (or have it at the same time and place after every sprint). It doesn't hurt to create a bit of pressure for the team.

7.1.3 It's Fun to Finish Things

Deadlines are good for the team as well. It is much more fun to clean the board, throw away the stories, wipe out the sprint burn-down chart, and start over with a fresh new sprint planning meeting than to linger on the old stories. It gives a feeling of accomplishment to clean the old stuff, and excitement to start the new. The clearer your boundary between old and new is, the better the feeling.

7.2   Don't Let Deadlines Woosh By

The team's demo was scheduled for Friday, but on Wednesday Jeff was still investigating the performance improvement that didn't work. When Laura asked his help for the synchronization feature, they suddenly realized they couldn't do both; but with the performance improvement implemented only halfway, actually nothing was working at the moment.

At the end of Thursday, Jeff finally checked in his code. But now the reporting was broken. And fifty-odd tests failed. And the demo was tomorrow morning.

It's not easy to meet your deadline. It requires discipline to really finish your work and good planning to do that at the set time. The good thing about Scrum is that you will have deadlines often—you get a lot of opportunity to gain experience.

7.2.1 Minimize Work in Progress

To have a clear and simple demo, your work needs to be done. If a story or task is really done, it's usually easy to demo it. If it is just nearly done, it can be very difficult to show: You don't have a clean install, you have to work around unimplemented bits, or it fails in front of the audience. So the key to a good demo is to finish all your work. Now how do you make sure your work gets done?

It helps a lot to have clear focus. Work on as few tasks in parallel as possible. Finish a story before you take on the next one. Each finished story makes a good demo; each additional story in progress is not helping another one being finished.

7.2.2 Don't Commit to Too Much Work

It sounds obvious, but it can't be repeated often enough: Don't take on more work than you can do. Be very strict in what you can take into your sprint. Don't fool yourself and don't fool your stakeholders.

It may be tempting to take in more work, because it will please your stakeholders. But they will no longer be pleased if the work isn't done in the end. If you know you cannot finish all the work from the beginning, you will lose focus on the work you can do. And then you will end up with a lot of stories started, but none finished.

7.3   On with the Show

"Well, guys, we have our sprint demo tomorrow. What are we going to show?"

"We have the new service implemented, but we cannot really show that, because the client isn't ready yet. Then we did the performance measurements, but the tests took three days to run, so we cannot demo that. And we fixed the display bug! But that was already released to production, so we cannot show the difference with the old display, because we don't have that anymore. I can mock up some screenshots . . ."

Some features are easy to demo and some are not. If you created a new button that does something, pressing the button in front of the audience is a convincing demo; they can see what it looks like, how it works, and, not unimportant, that it works.

But how do you demo something difficult? The key is to realize who your audience is: your stakeholders. They understand the feature because they need it, so there is not a lot to explain. The most important thing to show in a demo is that it works.

7.3.1 It Starts at the Planning

Preparing for a good demo actually starts at the planning already. If you write a user story that is easy to demo, it probably has good business value: It is a real feature, a solution to a problem that users have and recognize. If it is difficult to demo, chances exist that it is not a good feature: It is too technical, it is groundwork for a real feature, or it is just not very interesting.

So thinking about a future demo shapes your user story. But it shapes your user story in a good way: Features that bring tangible value for the user are good features. If your effort just delivers ground work, or architecture, or preparation for a real feature, you might be spending too much time on preparation that you can spend on business value instead. It is better to start with the business value and do the prerequisite work as part of a user story that describes a clear feature.

Ask yourself this question during the planning already: Is it easy to demo? If so, it is a good feature, and your demo will be easy.

7.3.2 Make a Demo Plan

Although finished stories are usually easy to demo, that doesn't mean your demo comes for free. It is a good idea to start thinking about what you can finish after three-quarters of your sprint and about what you can demo 1 or 2 days in advance. After all you will be presenting it for a room full of people.

But don't overdo the preparation. It is better to spend time on finishing the work instead. Do the minimal amount of planning to come to the demo meeting well prepared: Decide what to demo, decide who does what, and find out what you need.

Have a quick meeting with the team to come up with a *demo plan*: For each story, decide how to demo it and what needs to be prepared. Let the team decide who will prepare and demo what; if everybody picks a story to demo, the preparation can be quick and in parallel. Testers can do good demos sometimes by just running the tests, if the tests can be followed and understood by the audience. If you can get your users to demo a new feature it is even better!

Some demos are best done in pairs. One person does the clicking and typing, while the other one talks. This makes both the clicking and typing and the talking more fluent. It is difficult to do both at the same time. It also forces you to think a bit about your demo in advance, instead of improvising completely.

Make sure you have a nice introduction and you know what to show and what to tell. Check out the room where you have the demo for availability of a projector, a screen, network cables, wall outlets, or anything else you might need.

7.3.3 Avoid PowerPoint

Presentations are nice, but demos are much nicer. Don't show a picture of what a screen looks like if you can show the screen itself. The most boring demos are endless presentations about what has been done without showing the actual result. Think again: What are you showing on those slides? Can you show it in real life?

There is a time and place for everything, even for PowerPoint. You can use it for a short introduction about your sprint, showing the stories done and maybe some statistics, and you can use it if you have tables and graphs of test results, for instance. But always value demo over presentation.

7.3.4 Wiki Pages for Demos and Sprints

Do you have a wiki for your documentation already? All your statistics and information about Scrum can also go onto your wiki, and you can also use it for test data and test results. Then you can show the wiki pages during the demo, and they will not get lost afterwards.

Wikis are good for keeping track of your sprints, just like they are for documentation:

- Wikis won't go away and are in one, centralized place.
- It is easy to fill the wiki as the sprint progresses, instead of creating a presentation just before the demo.
- You can work together with several people on a wiki, easier than on loose documents.
- You can use a wiki for much more: design sketches, documentation, and manuals, the product backlog, team members' details, and so on.

Wikis and Scrum fit together very well.

7.3.5 Shorter Is Better

Demos don't have to fill the entire meeting that you allocated for it. If you can show some working software in 5 minutes, you did a fantastic demo.

Do you write client and server software? Then it is very well possible you can demo two (or more) stories with one press of a button. If you can show what the user will experience, there is no need to explain what is happening behind the scenes.

Save the time to answer questions from the audience. Or even better, save the time to have the audience themselves play with the new feature. There is one thing even better than *demoing* working software to people: *giving* working software to people.

7.3.6 Let's Look at a Detailed Example Again

For an example of a good demo, let's look at the board game server again: an online web-based service where you can play chess, checkers, and bridge. The team implemented the following user story:

As a player, I want to see who is online, so I can find my friends.

A convincing demo would look like this: open a browser and navigate to the URL of the game server. Click on the link that brings you to the list of other players and see that nobody is there. Now someone else logs in to the game server from another computer, and the audience sees this person appearing in the list. If they log out again, they disappear from the list.

Maybe you can share the location of the game server with the audience and they can all log in and out to see it working. That would be even more convincing.

Now the team shows a wiki page containing the results of a load test and mentions the conclusion that with the current hardware and software, 5,000 concurrent users can be handled.

Note that it is not necessary to show how this is all done. You only have to show working software.

7.4   Sprint Flow

A good planning, a fixed-size sprint, a nice demo, those ingredients will lead to a happy *sprint flow*. The team will get used to a rhythm in each sprint. First, you get acquainted to the work to be done, think, design, and find solutions. In the middle period, most of the work is done. And last, you tie up all loose ends and deliver the working software. The sprint flow is actually quite soothing. In each period, you know what is expected. And except for the last few days, there is little time pressure.

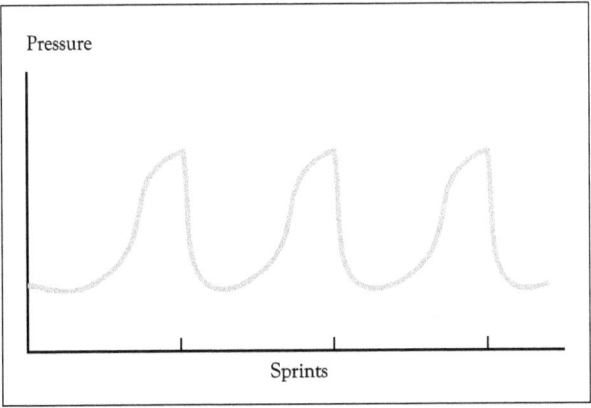

Figure 7.2 The waveform of sprints

You can make a graph of the pressure, or the work load, in a sprint over time, as done in Figure 7.2. Each phase has its characteristics; together it forms the waveform of sprints. The predictability of the phases makes the team very productive. There is time pressure, but not too much of it; there is no uncertainty about what needs to be done. There is a period of just working that is short enough not to become boring or unfocussed. And after that, you celebrate with a demo, you make the stakeholders happy and well informed by showing them working software, and then you look back and improve.

Demos play a key role in this. The pressure in the team builds up because they know they need to do a demo. And the feeling of accomplishment afterwards is much stronger when you show your work to your stakeholders. This sets the team up for a good retrospective and another successful sprint.

7.5   Sprint Demos: Getting It Right

"Where's your demo? Weren't you supposed to do a demo?"

"We had that five minutes ago. But here's the URL of our application. Try it out yourself!"

A good demo is nice to do; showing new and shiny features to stakeholders makes everyone happy. The key to a demo like that is that you are prepared for it.

To get into the habit of doing good demos, do it the same way every sprint:

- Schedule your demo meeting immediately at the beginning of the sprint.
- Minimize work in progress during the sprint.
- Make a demo plan: what to demo, how to demo it, and who will be demoing what.
- Show working software.
- And remember: Short is good.

Don't put a lot of time in preparing the demo meeting itself though. Prepare by carefully finishing your stories. That is what the demo meeting should be made of: demonstrating finished work.

And that is why it is always useful to have a demo. It gives you an incentive to *really* finish things. Only then it will be fun to demo it.

A very powerful side effect of demos is that they shape your sprint. They form the mark that the team is heading for all the way. And if done well, they are the exclamation marks that end the sentence on a high!

CHAPTER 8

Look Back!

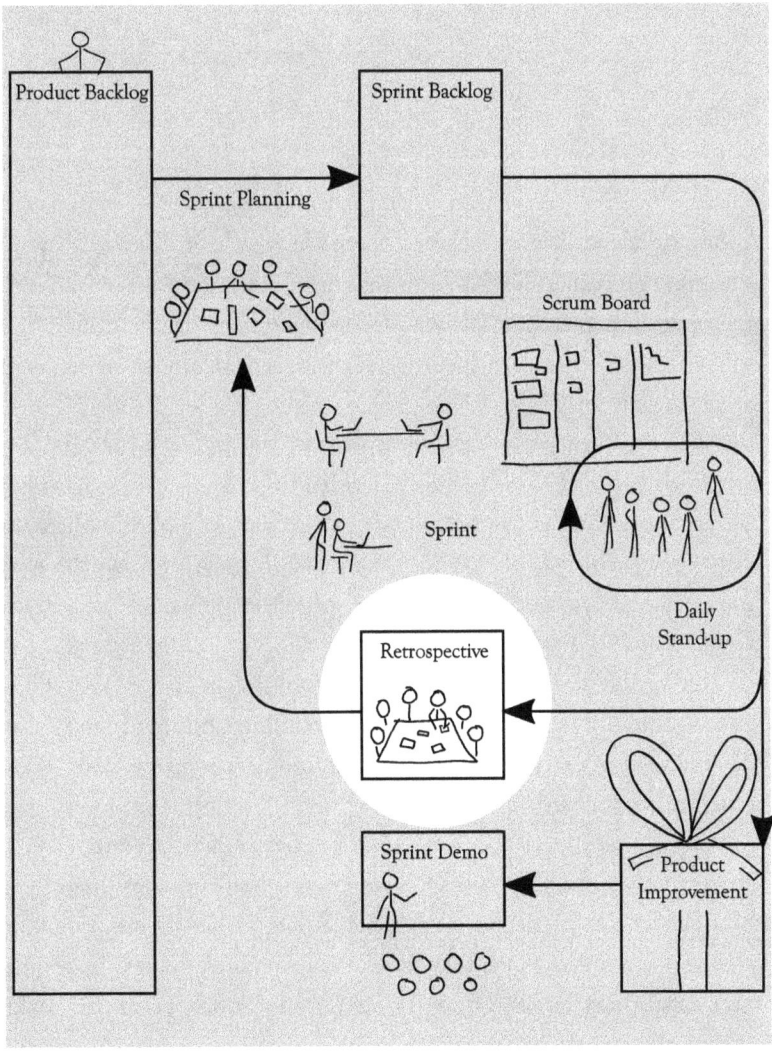

Figure 8.1 The sprint retrospective

The Team did a fantastic demo. Everything worked flawlessly, even that mocked up user interface that clearly showed that hidden feature. The audience seemed to understand the features shown, and approve of them—there even was a round of applause after the demo. The developers walk back to the team room with big smiles on their faces.

"Do we have a retrospective now?"

"Why have a retrospective? Everything went right, didn't it? No need to discuss what went wrong when everything went right!"

Right?

Wrong.

A long time ago in my company, when we were still making software for other companies, we did a project that turned into a disaster. Deadlines were not met, the software had lots of bugs, the customer was unhappy, and we had to spend a lot of time and money to set it all straight again.

After everything was over, the customer was happy again, and the developers had had some sleep, we decided to do a *postmortem* meeting: We sat down with all the people involved, trying to find out where we went wrong and how we could prevent this from happening the next time. After all, we hadn't enjoyed the experience and would rather learn from it than live it again.

During the meeting, it was proven that hindsight is always 20/20: It was easy to point out wrong decisions, bad timing, and coincidences that could have been prevented. So at a certain moment someone said: "Why didn't we do this earlier?"

An agile retrospective is a postmortem before it is too late. Henrik Kniberg writes in *Scrum and XP from the Trenches*: "The most important thing about retrospectives is *to make sure they happen*." And they shouldn't happen when it is too late; they should happen regularly. Ideally, you do them each sprint, as you can see in Figure 8.1. Now how can you make sure your retrospectives pay off?

8.1   Learn from the Past

The retrospective was skipped, and The Team happily started a new sprint. Again, they successfully delivered. Well, most of it. But the next sprint didn't go so well. The one after that was even worse.

Tim, the tester, was annoyed because his tests kept breaking because of architectural changes. Jeff was sitting in a corner working on his own stuff. Chris was picking up all the bugs and production issues that popped up. Jennifer didn't want to pair with Jeff, because they didn't get along very well. Stories on the Scrum board were re-written by the team members working on it, without discussion.

The list was endless. Not only were bad practices introduced over time, but good practices had been dropped as well. And nobody had noticed . . .

To learn from the past, you have to go over it and think about it. The retrospective offers you an opportunity to do that.

Even if everything went well, it is worth thinking about: Why did it go well? How can we repeat this success? So don't skip a retrospective because you're mostly happy about the last sprint. Good habits will be lost, and bad habits will build up. Long-time habits are much more difficult to fix.

8.1.1 Party Time!

The retrospective is an opportunity for celebrating after a successful sprint. It will make you feel up and ready for the next sprint. It doesn't have to be a full party with drinks, food, and music (although some cookies with the coffee may be nice) but patting yourselves on the back and congratulating each other with a successful demo is a good thing. Ideally, the retrospective is on the same day as the demo, to conclude the sprint looking back; then have the next sprint planning meeting the next (business) day, to start the new sprint looking forward. Having all three meetings on the same day can be done, but is a hard day of work.

8.1.2 Identify Problems You Had

The obvious things to discuss in a retrospective meeting are: What went wrong? What can we improve in the next sprint? But don't restrict yourselves to code-related issues. Think about the stand-up meetings, the demo, the releases (if any), distractions, availability of machines, sticky notes, whiteboards, the communication in the team—this is your opportunity to talk about anything that you didn't like in this sprint.

One goal of retrospectives is to improve the things that didn't go well. To improve them, you first have to get them on the table. So name them, list them, and make sure everything that wasn't good is mentioned.

8.1.3 No Blaming or Fingerpointing

Try to refrain from blaming or fingerpointing. Say "the Scrum board is falling apart" instead of "*you* promised to arrange for a new Scrum board." Say "I feel I don't get a lot of help"; don't say "I didn't finish it because *you* didn't answer my questions." Blaming people may make them feel bad and will probably make them act defensively, and then the discussion moves away from finding a solution to finding out who was at fault.

Try to see things as a team responsibility. By all means, mention what is wrong, but don't assume someone else should have fixed it. Try to explore the reason why it went wrong, instead of assuming you know already.

Taking the blame is another thing altogether. Saying "yes, that was my fault, I'll fix it" is clearly a good thing to do.

8.1.4 Repeat What You Did Right

What goes for problems also goes for good things: You have to identify them to be able to benefit from them again. So it is equally important to make a list of things that went well during the last sprint as it is to make the list of problems; it will be much easier to stick to them. And sticking to good habits is even more effective than trying to avoid bad habits.

Apart from that, what is a very good thing to some people might be a very casual thing for others. You might have forgotten you drew a quick diagram on the whiteboard that day, but someone else might mention it as a very good thing. That would be a good reason to draw more diagrams.

Last but not least: It feels good to make a list of good things. It is part of celebrating a successful sprint. That alone is a good reason to do it.

8.2   Every Beginning Is Difficult

The Team is sitting in the room for their first retrospective. As nobody knows what to say, Sam, the Scrum Master, begins.

"So it all went pretty well, didn't it?"

Nodding around the table.

"We didn't really have problems, apart from that story that was much more difficult than we expected?"

Silence.

"Well, let's call it a day then."

Does this retrospective meeting look familiar? Retrospective meetings are actually quite hard. For many people, they are unfamiliar territory, because you are talking about the process instead of about the work itself.

8.2.1 But I Don't Like Retrospectives!

Retrospective meetings can be pretty boring in the beginning, as nobody knows what to say. The team members might be too polite, not mentioning problems in an attempt to not offend anyone. And since nobody knows yet what is effective in retrospectives, the meeting might be over very soon.

The opposite usually comes later: endless ranting about how bad it all was, lots of discussion, and possibly lots of blaming and fingerpointing. Some retrospectives don't seem to end. The team comes out of the room exhausted, annoyed, and certainly not looking forward to the next sprint. They're not eager to have another retrospective meeting soon.

Still, a lot of good things are happening in those retrospectives. If you have a boring retrospective, things are going reasonably well. If you have a very heated retrospective, at least you find out the team is not very happy. The key to getting something out of retrospectives is to realize you always learn something from them. Try to list the things you learned at the end of the retrospective, to end on a slightly happier note.

8.2.2 Forming, Storming, Norming, Performing

In his articles about group development, "Developmental Sequence in Small Groups" and "Stages of Small Group Development Revisited," Bruce Tuckman described four stages of group behavior: forming, storming, norming, and performing (and a fifth one, adjourning). The idea is that a group goes through those stages in that order. First they get to know each other (forming); then they go through conflict, discussions, and competition when their personalities clash (storming). If they get through this stage, they will settle on the "rules" of the group (norming), after which they can really perform as a team.

The important insight Tuckman had is that all these phases always happen in this order: You cannot skip a phase. So to get to norming and performing, you *have* to go through the storming phase. The worst thing a team can do is to suppress all unpleasant thoughts and gripes they have about team performance, as it will never get them through to the next stage.

Retrospective meetings are a good tool to bring out the best in teams, as it will more or less force them to talk about how they work together. This will make it much easier to go through all the stages. Compared to teams that never look back, you will see the team spirit grow much faster.

8.2.3 Just the Team

Retrospectives are for the team only. The stand-up is open for everyone (although some may need to remain silent). The sprint planning is equally open (although nobody may want to attend it apart from the team) and the sprint demo is actually meant for everybody outside the team, but the retrospective is not. Team members will never speak freely if managers or stakeholders are around.

The Scrum Master is of course part of the team. The Product Owner is also part of the team. Business owners, product managers, or stakeholders aren't.

8.3 Get It on the Table

Jennifer had prepared for the meeting very well. She had a notebook full of notes with her, and when the meeting started, she took the floor.

"Right. First of all, I must say that pair programming really doesn't work for me. I mean, I tried to do it twice with Jeff, but he just types too slow and does everything with the mouse. Then I think we should have prepared the story about the database model a lot better. I mean, we must have changed it four times or so? And . . . no, let me finish, the user interface story was not better, because . . ."

In a retrospective, it is vital that everybody gets their say. Each team member may have a different opinion about what was good or not so good, so everybody must get the opportunity to speak.

But some people are better speakers than others; some like talking and some don't. To make sure the talkers don't drown out the others, there are some simple methods to try in retrospectives.

8.3.1 Do the Rounds

An easy way to do a retrospective is to go around the table and let every team member say one, and not more than one, thing that went well. You may pass if you cannot think of any. The Scrum Master (or someone else) writes them on sticky notes and sticks them to the wall where everyone can see them. After a full round of passes, go around the table and let every team member say one, and not more than one, problem in the sprint, until everyone passes. Stick them to the wall also. Pick a few items that need further discussion, preferably not more than three, and come up with some very easy, actionable ways to improve.

The advantage of going around the table this way is that every team member gets their say. It is not that the first speaker is stealing all the issues. It could still be a good idea to make the loudest team member go last.

Bring the Board

Even if the retrospective meeting is in another room, it might be a good idea to bring the Scrum board. Looking at the stories and the burn-down chart helps to remember how the sprint went.

8.3.2 Timeline Lists

You can also go over the sprint in chronological order. Draw a timeline on a whiteboard, start at the beginning, and add things that happened in the sprint on the timeline. Now discuss the items, moving good things that happened above the line and the problems below it. Then decide which items need more discussion.

Add the burn-down chart and other sprint-related data to the timeline, if that helps the team. Also bank holidays, releases performed, and other events can be added to the timeline. The timeline helps you to remember things and to make sure quiet team members get their say.

8.3.3 The Sailboat Retro and Other Questions

It can help to ask the question in a different way. In a sailboat retrospective, you don't ask what went well and what problems you encountered. Instead, you put a drawing of a sailboat on the wall, like in Figure 8.2.

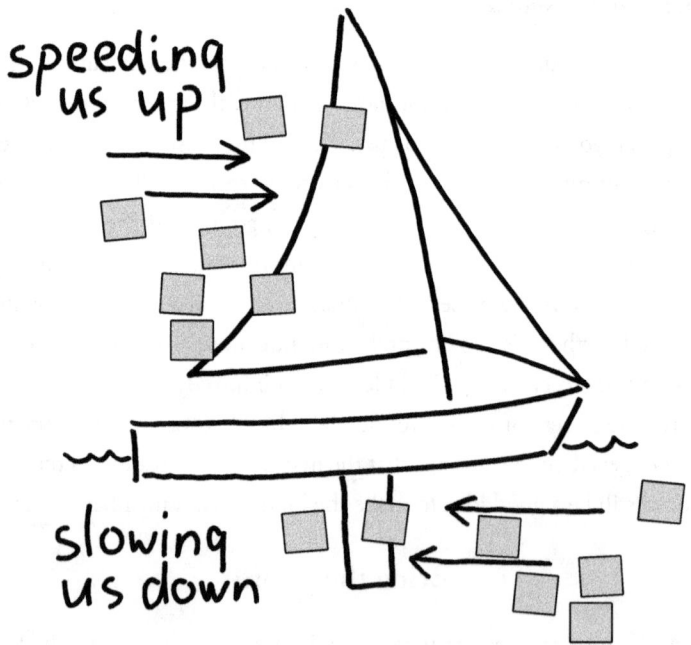

Figure 8.2 A sailboat retro

Now you ask: What made us move faster? Everything the team comes up with is written on a sticky note and put on the wall near the sail of the boat. Then you ask: What slowed us down? These items are stuck underwater, because the current and the water are slowing the boat down.

There are even more ways to ask the important questions:

- What made you glad?
- What made you mad?
- What made you sad?

. . . or

- What should we stop doing?
- What should we continue doing?
- What should we start doing?

Every set of questions serves the same purpose: Collect some information about how everyone felt that the sprint went. Varying the questions might help to keep your retrospectives going; if you always ask the same questions, it might become difficult to think of new things.

8.3.4 Writing Apart

One more method for listing things that went well and problems encountered in a retrospective meeting is by letting each team member, or groups of two or three team members, write down good things and problems encountered. Split the team up in groups of two or three and let every group write a bunch of sticky notes with good things and problems, for about 10 minutes, or let each individual team member do that. Then each group or person in turn puts the sticky notes on the wall, putting the ones that are the same (or very strongly related) together.

One advantage of this is that it is instantly clear which items deserve more discussion: They form the largest groups of sticky notes on the wall.

8.3.5 Dot Voting

If you have created a list of things that went well and a list of problems you encountered, it is time to discuss. If it is not obvious which items to discuss further, you can do *dot voting*: Using a marker, every team member can put three dots on items, possibly all three on one. The items with the most dots win.

Don't do dot voting if there are only a few items to discuss, and weed out the improvements that are blindly obvious (like "better handwriting on sticky notes" or "be on time in retrospective meeting"). For this type of improvements there is only one advice: Just do it.

Meeting by Phone

Retrospectives are probably the most difficult meetings to do with remote team members, because of all the discussions going on. If you can, try to make the remote team members come over for the retrospective (and maybe the planning meeting as well). If that can't be done, try to make the best of it.

- What goes for stand-up meetings by phone goes for retrospectives by phone as well: Be disciplined.
- Especially during the discussions at the end, don't forget the people on the other side of the line. If you don't use video, maybe you can have photographs or something else representing the people who are not present.
- If necessary, assign somebody the task of chairperson, who decides who may speak next. Normally you probably don't need a chair, since a Scrum team is not very large, but with remote members it may help.
- Decide on a (silent) signal people on the remote end can use to ask the chair for a turn. Especially when you have delays, if you just start to talk you will probably interrupt somebody.
- Be careful that a discussion doesn't create two parties, one on this side, one on the other. Everybody in the Scrum team is equal. If you see that this is happening anyway, talk about it and find out if this is really what people think, or that it is caused by the barrier between the groups. If that is the case, restart the discussion with this new insight.

8.4   Inspect and Adapt

"Guys, time is up. Here is the list of problems; Gary, can you hand me the good things? Thanks."

"But what do we do with these lists?"

Listing problems doesn't make them go away. Although it is important to get everything on the table, it is equally important to analyze the lists. In the end, you want some action items that will improve your next sprint.

8.4.1 Digging Down

It is important to discuss items a bit further. The aim is to find out *why* things went well or *why* things didn't go that well. The real *why* might be hidden deep under the surface. The trick is to dig down deep enough that you can find it.

Take a simple example: The most important story was not finished. There is one task belonging to that story that was in progress for the entire sprint. Why was that? It turns out that Chris, who worked on it, moved on to another task. Why was that? Because he was the expert on that subject and somebody asked for his help. And why didn't another team member pick it up then? Because other team members didn't know what the status of that task was. And Chris didn't check in the code he had written so far, because it wasn't finished yet and didn't compile without error.

Now we move from "the most important story wasn't finished" to "abandoned tasks can be hard to pick up," which is a lot easier to fix. Several solutions spring to mind:

- Never abandon a task.
- Always hand over tasks explicitly to someone else.
- Go over all tasks in progress during the stand-up to make sure progress is made.
- Always check in code at the end of the day, even if it is incomplete and breaks the build.

Whether these solutions are good remains to be seen, but they are much easier to do than "try to finish the most important story."

This method of digging down is known as *the five whys*, because it takes about five times asking "why" to get to the bottom. There are more ways to dig down, of course. The most important thing is that you do it. Try to go from a big and fuzzy problem to a small and clear one.

8.4.2 Improvement Items

Retrospective meetings should result in three or four *improvement items* or good resolutions for the next sprint. These items should be as specific as possible. Not "do more pair programming," but "Chris should always pair up." Don't say "try to talk more to the team," rather say "never move sticky notes in stand-up meetings." More specific is easier to do, and it is easier to see that you've really done it. And once you have done it for a full sprint, it will have become a habit.

Hide and Seek

In a retrospective after a sprint where none of the stories was completed, my team felt they had spread their attention over all the stories at once. Team members didn't work together on stories, but each picked their own which they couldn't complete alone.

To force the team to focus on fewer stories and to encourage working together, the team decided to postpone the breaking down in tasks. At the beginning of the sprint, just the two stories with the highest priority were broken down in tasks; only when a team member really couldn't work on any of the stories in progress, a team meeting was called and the next story was tasked. The team was much more focused, and team members tried much harder to pick up tasks from the top-priority stories.

A strange thing happened a few sprints later. The team found out that the last story in the sprint backlog wasn't completed, because no tasks were written. Nobody picked up the work because no tasks were readily available. The team changed their way of working again and tasked all stories at the beginning of the sprint. But by then, the habit to work on high-priority items first was strong enough that they didn't slip back into working on everything at the same time.

Don't be afraid to have strange improvement items, like "hide stories we're not working on." If it works for you, it's good. Also don't be afraid of improvements that are the direct opposite of earlier improvements, like "put all stories for this and the next sprint on the board." Teams change, people learn, and if you decide that it works for you, it's good.

8.4.3 Keep It to Yourself

Try not to place problems outside your team. "We didn't finish stories because there was too much unplanned work. That was not our fault." You still can do something to improve the situation:

- Take in less work and make sure you *do* finish that.
- Track and size unplanned work, so you get a better understanding of how much it is.
- Have the Product Owner push back harder when people from outside the team come up with things to do during the sprint.
- Of course it is a good idea to talk to the people that brought in all the unplanned work too.

This will maybe not make the unplanned work go away, but at least you try to solve the situation by doing things that you control. Don't get trapped in the idea that it is all someone else's fault. Even if this is true, you can try to improve in *handling* it.

8.4.4 Team Consensus

Deciding on improvement items is the most important part of the retrospective meeting. Here the team is agreeing on the things that will make the next sprint better. The team should reach consensus about those items, that is, they should all agree that these items are the most worthwhile things to try in the next sprint.

You don't reach consensus by majority vote, so don't use dot voting for this. You reach consensus only if every team member agrees that this is the best way *for the team* to go. If someone is really against it, you probably shouldn't do it. If someone really wants something, it's probably worth trying. This is not about the majority rule over the minority; this is about the whole team agreeing.

To reach consensus every team member needs to be open-minded, cooperative, and work toward a solution. Be patient. It can take a long time to reach consensus.

Why is team consensus so important? Because the team as a whole needs to actually *do* the things that were decided. If some members don't believe in it, they will not do it. If some team members don't do it, it probably won't work. And then the whole exercise was for nothing.

Retrospectives Getting Boring

After you have had a lot of them, retrospectives can get a bit boring. Improvements are no longer so easy to find, and the format of the meeting starts to get old. There are a few things you can do to breathe new life into your retrospectives.

- Have a meeting about a specific subject instead, for example, "using Git effectively" or "Meeting by phone." Ideally, the subject has something to do with your work process. It will be an interesting change and will still have retrospective quality.
- Change the format. Just choose another format from the ones described earlier or a different set of questions.
- Skip a retro. Just don't skip all of them . . . Reschedule your retro to 2 or 3 weeks later and have it then.

If the team starts dreading retrospectives, something needs to be changed, else your retrospectives are not effective. But *not* having retrospectives anymore is not a solution. Make sure you have them regularly, and make them count!

8.5   Retrospectives: Getting It Right

So The Team did a fantastic demo. Everything worked flawlessly, even that mocked up user interface that clearly showed that hidden feature. The audience seemed to understand the features shown, and approve of them—there even was a round of applause after the demo. The developers walk back to the team room with big smiles on their faces.

"The best thing this sprint really was how you and Jen mocked up that interface. That was such a smart way to demo the feature!"

"But to get the story finished to begin with! I never thought we could do that."

"I think this was the best sprint we had so far."

"What a sec, guys. Did you start the retrospective already?"

If your retrospectives are not effective, settle on some simple and playful methods to get the information on the table:

- Celebrate the end of the sprint. Bring cookies to make sure everybody comes!
- Try one of the retrospective formats described. Pick another one if it doesn't seem to work.
- Use the Five Whys to dig down.

Then come up with some simple, physical improvements. For example, make some changes on the Scrum board. Don't try to solve all problems at once. Settle on some simple solutions for small improvements, and take the time to make them work out.

Retrospectives can be scary, because it forces the team to talk about the process (and emotions and relationships) instead of work and code. And retrospective are difficult, as it can be hard to solve the problems found. Then they can also be boring when no one knows what to say. So start small. Make it easy. Many small changes can create big improvements.

Retrospectives are very important for team improvement. You cannot look forward all the time; sometimes you have to look back and learn. If your retrospectives are done honestly, seriously, and consistently, the team will improve. Take that opportunity: It is time well spent.

CHAPTER 9

Done, Done, Done, Done, Done

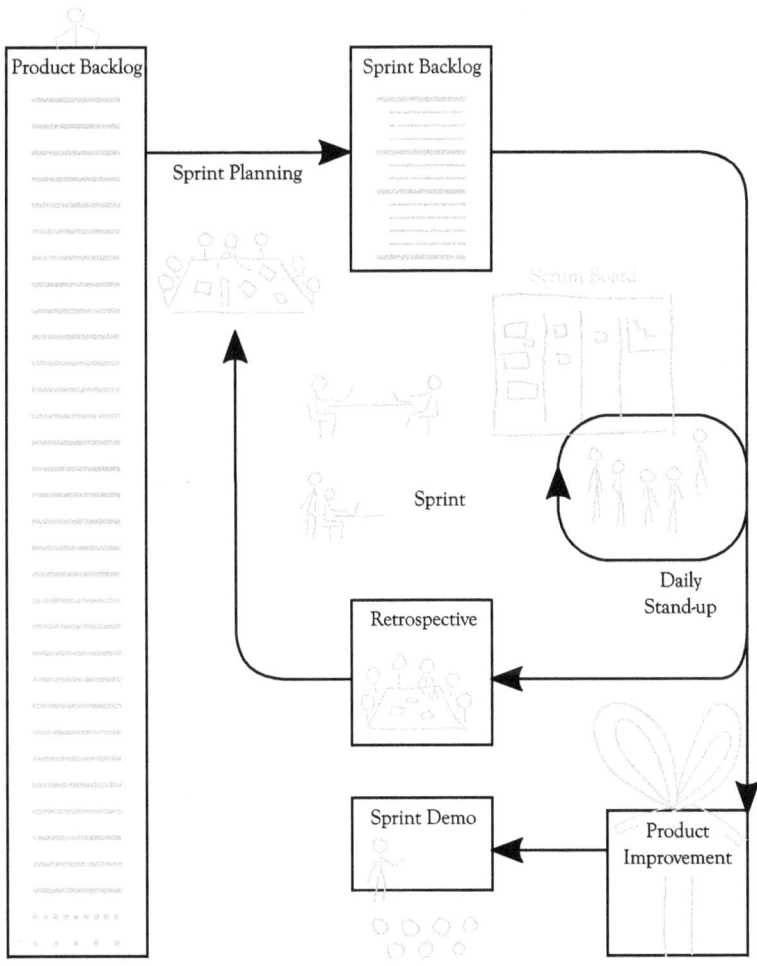

Figure 9.1 The Scrum process

The Team moved all stories (except the last one) to "Done." Quite a successful sprint that was! But in the next sprint, things didn't go so well. First of all, the new software still had to be integrated into the main product. Then they had to create the release packages to release the new software to production. They suddenly realized they hadn't planned for that.

So they adapted the plan, did the work, and went on with the new sprint. But then the bug reports started flowing in…

In a talk to Google, Jeff Sutherland, coinventor of Scrum, explains the evolution of the Definition of Done at PatientKeeper. First a feature was considered done when it was unit tested, but the stakeholders were not very happy with that. Then they said it was "done done" when it was system tested as well. They moved to "done done done" when it was acceptance tested by the users. It was "done done done done" when it was taken in production by at least four end users. But in the end, they settled for "done done done done done," if it was released to production for all the users they had. In Jeff's words: "Let's see if the phone rings in the next hour. That's our demo. And if the phone didn't ring, it was a *great* demo."

Although the Scrum process as shown in Figure 9.1 is clear and simple, it is not easy to perform it effectively. How can you make sure your software is "done done done done done," every time?

9.1   Definition of Done

"Is the login screen ready?"

"It's about 80% done."

It sounds odd to talk a lot about what *done* really means. After all, when it's done, it's done, isn't it? But actually it is well worth it to spend some time on the team's *Definition of Done*.

9.1.1 The More Done, the Better

Is your software ready when it passes all tests? Does that include integration tests, if it is part of a larger system? Was it tested by actual users? And does it really work in real life, on end users' machines?

Anything that is not part of your Definition of Done still needs to be done sooner or later. PatientKeeper invested a lot of time in advancing their Definition of Done as far toward the end user as possible. That way you exchange as much unplanned work for planned work as possible.

9.1.2 Done Includes Testing

If it is not practical, or even not possible, to release to production at the end of your sprint, your Definition of Done should include as much testing as possible. Just unit testing is not enough; system testing or end-to-end testing needs to be done also. If at all possible, acceptance testing should be part of the sprint as well.

If you don't do all levels of testing, the stories that were considered done will come back into a next sprint, because bugs or omissions will be found. When they come back then depends entirely on people outside your team and the urgency of it as well. But in the meantime, the team moved on and might be working on something different.

Just like your Definition of Done, your test strategy might need a lot of work. Make sure you pay it the attention it deserves.

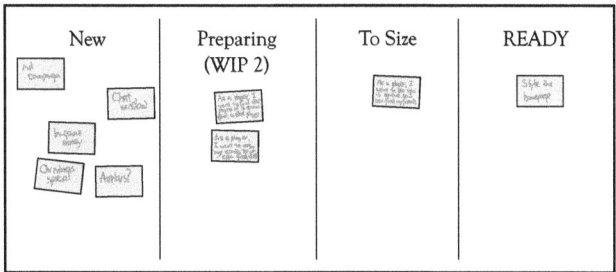

Figure 9.2 A Product Owner's KanBan board

Flow to READY, Iterate to Done

Not only is the Definition of Done an important thing to agree about in the team, also your Definition of Ready counts: When is a story ready to go into the sprint? As a team you should understand and agree on when a story can be considered READY: when all prerequisites are fulfilled and enough is known about it that the team can start working on it.

Serge Beaumont gives a good description on how you can visualize your stories getting READY in his blog post *Flow to READY, Iterate to DONE*. Use a KanBan board for the various stages your stories go through, from inception, through feasibility analysis and adding detail, to READY. The READY column then is your product backlog.

An example is shown in Figure 9.2. Stories that are just new go into *New*; when the Product Owner starts working on something it goes into *Preparing*. If the story is good enough for the team to size, it is moved to *To Size*; after sizing it is READY.

The stories flow from column to column continuously. The Product Owner can restrict the number of items he or she works on in parallel (the *Work In Progress* or WIP) by setting a *WIP-limit* of, for example, two stories. This makes sure progress is visible and stories don't get stuck without noticing, because you don't allow yourself to start working on something new before something else is moved to make place.

9.2   What Sizes Are Not

"So, how many story points can your team do?"

"Well, last sprint we did 12."

"And what's the size of that story? Eight? I'll give it to Robert's team then. They do 40 story points each sprint."

Story points are a useful tool for a Scrum team: They help you in estimating how much work you can do in an organized manner, and they allow your Product Owner to make a release plan that goes further into the future than just one sprint. When the team has a good Definition of Done and stories are truly READY before going into the sprint, you will find that their velocity is pretty stable. And with a stable velocity you can predict progress reasonably well.

But don't take story points and velocity for more than just a tool. Using story points will not make bad teams good, and pushing velocity to be as high as possible will not make your team faster. And comparing velocity between teams doesn't mean anything at all.

9.2.1 Velocity Is Different for Each Team

You cannot compare velocity between teams. Each team has their own strengths and weaknesses, so if a story is passed on to another team, the team needs to size the story again. If you size stories in ideal days you might be tempted to go with another team's size, but you shouldn't. The other team might have different expertise and a different approach to the story. But also sizing a story with the team means the team will understand the story, so it will not be a complete surprise when it comes into the sprint. When you are using story points instead of ideal days, it will be more obvious you have to size the stories again, since another team's story points are meaningless to you.

9.2.2 Focus Factor

The focus factor of the team shows how much the team can do per man-day. The easiest way to explain this is by an example.

Assume team A can do 20 story points in a 3-week sprint (their velocity is 20). The team consists of 5 people, so the availability (in working days) of the team is 5 people $\times$ 5 days $\times$ 3 weeks = 75 days. This means they do 20 $\div$ 75 or 0.27 story points per available man-day. This number (0.27) is called the focus factor.

The focus factor is a useful number for the team to compare sprints, because it factors out the number of man-days. Assume there are some holidays in the next sprint or some people not present, you can multiply the number of man-days with the focus factor to get a reduced velocity for that sprint. Don't overuse it though; if half of the team is gone, including your database specialist and your only tester, don't assume your velocity is going to be half that of last time. It will be much less.

9.2.3 Universal Velocity Is a Myth

It might be tempting to come up with the concept of *universal story points* that allow you to compare teams. And actually, it is pretty easy to do. But if you do the math, you'll see it's a rather useless exercise.

Let's look again at team A that has a velocity of 20 and a focus factor of 0.27. Now take team B. Their velocity is 50, but this team consists of only four people, with one of them being a part-timer. Why is their velocity so high? Not because they are much better, but their story points are much smaller.

Remember how we started using story points? Take a medium-sized story and assign a size to it, then size all other stories in comparison to that one. Here team A took a medium-sized story and gave it a 3, but team B took a story of roughly the same size and assigned it size 13. Neither of them is wrong; Team A will probably not use numbers above 8 a lot; team B will not have a lot of stories of size 1. But the relative size of all their stories is similar.

Another way to explain the difference is to look at the focus factor of both teams. Team B's availability is 3 people × 15 days, + 1 × 9 days, makes 54, so their focus factor is 50 ÷ 54 or 0.93, more than three times as high as that of team A.

But if you look at the average amount of work each team member has done per day, we can say that the 0.27 units of work done in team A equals the 0.93 units of work in team B, if everyone is working equally hard. To equalize velocity, we can both set them to 1 and adjust the story points accordingly.

Now the velocity of team A = 20 ÷ 0.27 = 75 and that of team B is 50 ÷ 0.93 = 54. Surprise: The velocity of both teams is equal to their availability. If you think about it, it makes total sense. If each team is working equally hard, then their "productivity," or the amount of work they do per day, is always going to be equal to their availability.

So if you wanted to compare the performance of teams by comparing their velocity, think again. You're only comparing availability, and there are easier ways to that. The only velocity you should compare to is your own velocity in the past.

9.2.4 Don't Push It

It seems clear that a higher velocity is desirable: If you do more story points per sprint, you get the work done faster, isn't it? But beware of pushing too hard on the velocity of your team.

If having a high velocity is so important, the team will be tempted to size stories larger. They might even do that without realizing it, because they just feel that "5" doesn't sound like a lot for a story that is rather large. If this happens, your long-term planning is not accurate anymore.

But even worse, the team may declare a story *done* even when it is not, because if they don't, their velocity will be lower. Over time, you will find that software quality decreases, and extra time is spent in rework and bug-fixing. So all you did is exchange some planned work for unplanned work.

9.3   Don't Plan for the Unknown

"I want you to keep detailed time sheets of all hours you spent on production problems."

"But why?"

"Because if we don't know how much time we lose, we cannot plan."

"But why?"

"Because if we don't know how much time we lose, we don't know how much time is left for real work."

"But it will show in our velocity!"

You can never predict the future (reliably anyway) but you can remember the past. In Scrum, the past is conveniently condensed into one number: your velocity. Your velocity does not only account for the work you planned to do, but also for the unplanned work you did. And that gives you the necessary bit of flexibility to tackle the unknown.

9.3.1 Dealing with Bugs

Even if "done" means *released to production* in your team, you still can't be 100% sure a finished story won't come back to you. However well tested, bugs might be discovered after the release. And bugs in production software usually have a very high priority.

Incoming bugs almost always disrupt your sprint. There is little you can do about it. The best thing you can do with it is handle it as all other unplanned work: Make a sticky note for it, put it on the board, give it the priority that is necessary ("should we drop everything of our hands *right now* or can we finish lunch first?"), and let the team pick it up.

The worst thing you can do with bugs is trying to ignore them. The work will pile up and then it will kill your sprint completely.

9.3.2 Planned versus Unplanned

All those unplanned items look ugly on your Scrum board. And they are not really prioritized, or sized, or handled top to bottom, as other items are. Why are unplanned items handled so sloppily in a neat and organized system like Scrum?

First of all: Unplanned items are, well, unplanned. You didn't plan for them. The fact that you even have a place for them on the board is already pretty organized. You have to make sure though that they deserve the status of unplanned: They should have high enough priority to be allowed to disrupt your sprint, and they should be small enough not to kill it completely. If a task is not really urgent, put it off till next sprint. If it is so large that you cannot expect to finish it within weeks, but it has to be done now, terminate the sprint and do a new planning session.

Once you have accepted an unplanned item in your sprint, what's next? Do it now. Then it's gone. The unplanned items area in effect is above all other stories on the Scrum board: It has the highest priority. If you handle unplanned items immediately, they have the smallest impact on your sprint.

9.3.3 Your Velocity Will Create Buffer Time

Handling unplanned items takes time; if you do a lot of unplanned work, you will do less planned work. In other words: The team's velocity will go down.

Hopefully, the amount of unplanned work per sprint is more or less stable. It grows a bit after a big release and shrinks a little in the holiday season, but that is all difficult to predict (it's *unplanned* after all). Small variations don't really matter; on average, your velocity will remain the same.

If you have lots of unplanned work in one sprint and very little in another, that is a reason for concern. Where does it come from and why does it come in bursts? This is a good topic for the retrospective.

If you have a lot of unplanned items on average, the variance between sprints will probably be large, meaning your velocity will jump up and down. That is not a good thing, because the predictability of the team will suffer. That is a good reason to keep the number of unplanned items as low as possible. If your amount of unplanned work is small enough, it will have little impact on your sprint. By using your velocity when planning a new sprint, you will automatically create buffer time for unplanned work.

To summarize: Plan everything you can, but don't bother about the things you cannot plan. Keep a close eye on unexpected things that happen during the sprint, and take a conscious decision on how to handle them: Do it now, put it off till later, or terminate the sprint and replan.

9.3.4 Too Much to Handle

But what if you can clearly see that the amount of unplanned work is too much to handle? If it is so much, or so late, that you know you will not be able to finish the last story in your sprint?

Deal with it. Either you size the work and remove the last story from your sprint, or you terminate the sprint and do a new planning. Don't start the work and hope for the best, if you can already predict that it will fail.

If you remove the last story (or one of the last few) from your sprint, your Product Owner can take action: Adjust the plans, inform the stakeholders, reorganize the work. If you replan, the Product Owner also has a new plan to work with. That is far better than finding out at the end of the sprint that some work wasn't done. The earlier you know that something is not going according to plan, the more time you have to deal with it; that goes not only for your Product Owner, but also for your stakeholders and customers.

9.3.5 Find the Source

If you have a lot of unplanned work, it is important to investigate where it all comes from. The sources of unplanned work can be very different:

- Low software quality, so lots of urgent bugs
- Problems with scalability or infrastructure
- Sudden rush jobs
- Operational work done by the development team
- General lack of focus by the team

This is a good subject for a retrospective. Can you identify the source of the unplanned work? And if so, is there a way to put it to a halt? It might need an investment in time, but sometimes you can structurally reduce unplanned work.

9.4   Sharpening the Saw

"How do you generate the daily report?"

"We create that manually."

"Why don't you write a program to do that for you?"

"We don't have time."

"Why don't you have time?"

"Because of all the reports we have to create manually . . ."

Even though you have a bit of leeway, large amounts of unplanned work should be avoided. But how can you avoid something that you don't know yet?

9.4.1 Invest in Tools

Apart from bugs, another source of unplanned work is lack of automation. If you have manual tests, manual setup work, manual deployments, or manual database maintenance, and the team is responsible for those, this will require a lot of time. Automated tools take even more time to create, but that will pay off later. Tools will make tedious work easier, make it easier to repeat those jobs, and ideally will allow the team to let someone else do the work.

Writing tools is work that can just be planned in; create a story for it and do it. This is a form of *sharpening the saw*, as Stephen Covey calls it in *The 7 Habits of Highly Effective People*: Don't get caught in boring and time-consuming work, if investing a little bit more time can get rid of it. Planning the creation of a tool is easy and predictable. Manual work is much harder to plan, and it can come back frequently.

9.4.2 Firefighters

If the amount of operational work is high, either because of buggy software or because your tools aren't mature enough, it may be better to split off part of your team into a new team, the *firefighters*.

While they take care of all operational work, the rest of the team can work in peace. The fire squad's main focus is to fix bugs and build tools; if they do that right, maybe they can be merged back into the team later. Seat the firefighters team near the door of your team room. They will form a human shield for distractions that way.

It might be difficult to merge the firefighters back into the development team. If the work for the firefighters is not much fun, you might rotate the team members every sprint or every few sprints, so everyone takes a fair share of uninteresting work.

9.4.3 Component Teams versus Feature Teams

Some teams don't work independently, but work on a component of a larger system. They can do unit testing, but for system testing they depend on other teams: Each component needs to be finished and the integration work has to be finished. Only then the system testing, acceptance testing, and release can be done.

This is a difficult situation. It is almost guaranteed that bugs will be found, bits will be missing, and help will be needed. But the team can never properly plan that, as the timing depends on other teams. So a lot of unplanned work will be generated.

Furthermore, this structure will lead to a lot of managerial overhead. For each new feature that is planned, the Product Owner of the team needs to deal with the Product Owners of other teams to synchronize the schedules. Instead of people being on the critical path, you now have complete teams on the critical path, for every single new feature.

A different approach for working in component teams is to form *feature teams*. A feature team is responsible for a new feature and will change every component that needs to be changed to implement it.

Having feature teams will get rid of unnecessary critical paths. The team itself will do everything necessary to implement the new feature and will not have to wait for other teams. It can also have a very advanced Definition of Done, because the team can consider the feature done when it is released to production. After all, they implement it all the way.

It does require something from the teams though: They will need to learn something from each system; and they will need to work together with all other feature teams that might work on the same components. It will probably take some time before the teams work smoothly together. Automated testing is vital to get it right. But in effect, you are exchanging managerial overhead for a technical challenge. And by the time you have real feature teams, they are more or less interchangeable. This will reduce the managerial overhead to a minimum.

If you have component teams, the change to feature teams is a large reorganization and can be difficult to realize. A possible way to form your initial feature teams is to take one member from each component team and put it in each feature team. That way each feature team will have a component expert, so each team as a whole has the knowledge necessary to implement a feature.

9.5   The End User's Done: Getting It Right

The Team moved all stories (except the last one) to "Done." Quite a successful sprint that was! And the only reason the last story wasn't done was because it was the Christmas Special Website. That could only be released to production on Christmas Eve, and that was still six weeks away.

And since Done meant "released to production" for the Team, they couldn't call it done.

Why is it so important to pay so much attention to the Definition of Done? Because your end users have only one Definition of Done: It Just Works. Perfectly. Anything short of that will make the end user unhappy, so they will come back and haunt you (or leave you for a competitor).

So work on your Definition of Done and see how far you can go. Buy yourself time by automating recurring tasks, and use that time to get rid of even more recurring work. And if it is possible, make your team responsible for the entire development track of a feature, from its inception to its release.

A good Definition of Done will not reduce the amount of work; that will remain the same. But it will keep the work together, instead of spreading it over the course of time. That will make it easier for the team to do it. Also, the better your Definition of Done, the more accurate your estimate is of the work that lies ahead of you, and that is what planning is all about.

In the end, all software becomes "done done done done done." The question is how far ahead you could see it coming.

CHAPTER 10

Power to the Team

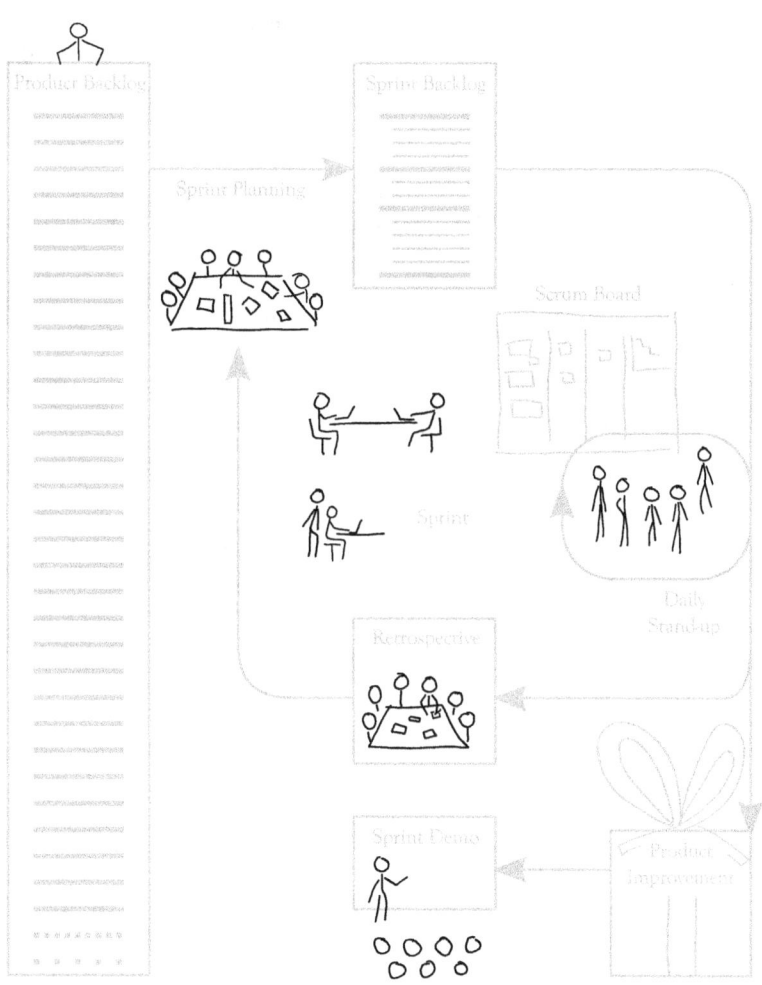

Figure 10.1 The Scrum team

"Now The Team is doing Scrum, and it works well: our schedule is clear and dependable, our code has high quality, and our production is going up. How can we keep this up?"

—The Team

A couple of months before we were going to show the first TomTom GO device to the world, we were still working hard to finish the software. We weren't doing Scrum yet in those days—we just did some sort of "Project Management by Common Sense."

We created a biweekly meeting for the team leads of the several teams that were working on the project, to report about progress and align where necessary. But when the deadline came nearer, it became weekly meeting, then every few days.

One question that Pieter Geelen, one of the owners of the company, would frequently ask is: "Without that feature, do we still have a product?" And if the answer to the question was "No," we would leave it and concentrate on more important parts first, the parts for which the answer to the question was "yes."

That was real agile management support: Prioritize rigorously, deliver the most important features first, and don't move deadlines. (We couldn't anyway.) And indeed, many of the features that we had in mind for the first device were only present in the second version that was released a year later. We could never have done that in the available time.

When doing Scrum, management support is important. Most importantly, the organization needs to understand how you are working, and adapt to that. But if you as a Scrum team prove that you are delivering high-quality software at a predictable schedule, you build trust in your team that makes the organization adapt to you. If your management sees that what you do is working, they will leave you to it, and then self-organizing teams will start to shine. It is the team, as shown in Figure 10.1, that makes or breaks the process.

Scrum is not a very complex method. There are only few things you have to do and some simple rules to follow. *Not complex* is not the same as easy though. It takes a great deal of effort and attention to do it right.

You are doing Scrum; the only thing left to learn is to be effective at doing Scrum. And that requires the team to be aware of what they are doing and to be confident that they are doing the right thing. A confident team will commit with confidence, work with confidence, and deliver with confidence, and thus will be a dependable team within an organization.

How do you become such a team? What properties does an effective Scrum team have that sets them apart?

10.1   The Product Owner's Role

The Team was happily coding when Joe from Marketing hopped in.

"Can you do me a favor? We have this big event next week and it would be really great if we could show the new user interface…"

The Team explained that they were already fully booked until next week Friday, but Joe wasn't sent away that easily.

"What? The performance story? That really can wait until after the show. If we don't sell our product, who cares about performance anyway?"

Then the phone rang: their biggest customer had a problem generating reports.

Charlie sighed. "This is all very important. But is there anyone who can decide what we should do next?"

The Product Owner is responsible for the product backlog. Do you have a Product Owner? If not, assign one.

10.1.1 What the Product Owner Does

Technically, the Product Owner does the following:

- Write user stories (or have them written).
- Have them sized.
- Order them by business value.

In practice, there is a whole lot more a Product Owner has to take care of: Keep an eye on what is happening in the company, so you can see user stories coming; chase stakeholders to get more detailed requirements from them; bring stakeholders together so they can discuss priorities between them.

Apart from that, the Product Owner must be able to answer all questions the team asks. The better he or she can do that, the faster the team can move; if the team has to chase each stakeholder for questions they cannot work very well.

Ideally, the Product Owner has enough authority to make decisions about priority as well. Of course he or she should consult with the stakeholders about priorities, but if, for example, during a sprint planning a spot decision is necessary, the Product Owner should be able to take it.

If the Product Owner is doing it right, the team is shielded from interruptions of the stakeholders completely. Stakeholders can talk to the Product Owner at any time; the Product Owner talks to the team when the time is right.

10.1.2 Velocity Is the Only Performance Measurement

The only measurement that is taken of the team's performance is velocity. It is no use measuring the hours of work spent by a certain person on a certain task. Working on stories is a team effort, and sizing stories is done by the team, so the only important piece of empirical data is the relation between them: how many story points can the team do. Chasing individual's hours is not going to change the amount and provides little useful data.

In effect, it even works counterproductive. Assume Jennifer is working on a task, but now Chris asks for help. This is really going to mess up Jennifer's time sheet. Either she doesn't book the time she helped Chris, making it look like she spent way more time on her task, or she decides to book half an hour here and three and a half hour there, giving her more work filling in the sheets. Or she decides that it is easier that someone else helps Chris.

And what do you have in the end? In the best possible case, a time sheet that shows that everyone has worked all their available time on some tasks. But that you have found out anyway by the end of the sprint.

If you need to come up with a sheet of person-hours spent per feature or project, you can divide the number of story points of a finished story by the focus factor. This will give you the number of person-days the team worked on that story.

10.1.3 Release Planning

If you know the team's velocity and you have sized backlog items in advance for a couple of sprints, you can very easily derive a *release plan* from it. If you order the backlog by priority, you can chop it into sprint-sized chunks. And then, for every story in the backlog, you can see at what date it is likely finished, as sprints have a fixed length. From this plan you can determine when a release can be made and what will be in it. Of course you have to account for some uncertainty, as velocity is an average number.

If your sprint history is long enough, you can derive the worst case velocity and best case velocity by taking the average of a few of the slowest sprints and a few of the fastest. Using those two velocities you can derive the earliest and latest release date based on actual team performance. As more work gets done and the time to the release becomes shorter, this release interval will shrink, until it is contained in one sprint. You can make a graph that will show this interval clearly: This is called a *release burn-down*. Figure 10.2 shows an example of this.

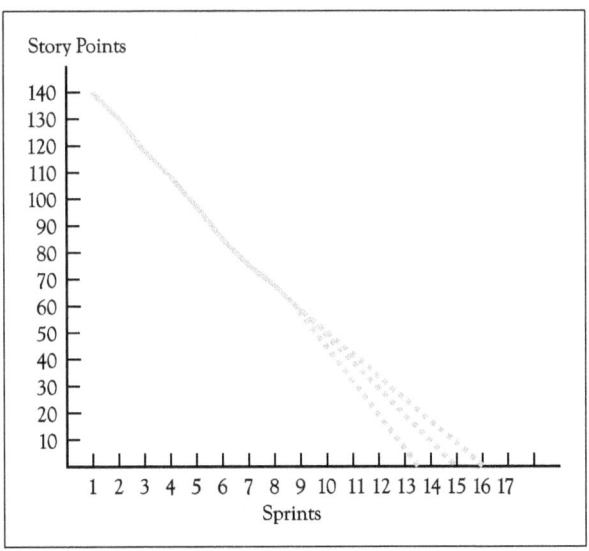

Figure 10.2 A release burn-down

On the vertical axis, you see the total number of story points for the project. On the horizontal axis you plot the sprints. After every sprint, you can add a piece to the graph.

The dotted lines are the predicted burn-down graphs using the worst velocity from the last few sprints, the average velocity, and the best velocity. From these lines you can predict in which sprint the product will likely be ready. Over time, the predicted sprints will come closer together, until they end up in the same sprint, and then you know when the project will be finished.

The remainder of the release plan becomes more accurate over time. If the team's velocity changes or the backlog changes, the release plan will change; but while more stories get done, fewer stories are left, and the average velocity becomes more reliable. This works together in making the rest of the plan more accurate.

10.1.4 Own and Share the Release Plan

It is up to the Product Owner to translate the release plan to whatever the organization expects. But since the release plan is both reliable and flexible, it should fit any organization's needs.

The nice thing about this release plan is that you can change it anytime by reordering the backlog, without disrupting the team. Product Owners can align the backlogs of several teams to make product- or program-release plans far into the future, but the plan is never fixed for more than the current sprint. This is a flexible way of roadmap planning that is based on facts, not guesses.

There are a few things that can make a release plan like this difficult or imprecise. One of them is a sloppy Definition of Done. If finished stories are not really finished, you can expect a lot of unplanned work and thus a very inconsistent velocity.

Another thing to beware of is late user stories. If the user stories are not known well in advance and if the stakeholders bring in many new user stories the day before the sprint planning, your release plan changes every sprint. It is up to the Product Owner to hunt down user stories as early as possible; but if the plans of the organization change very frequently, you still cannot plan very far in advance. But that is regardless of the planning method used.

10.1.5 Technical Stories

Once in a while you spot a problem in your project that is too large to fix immediately or that is entirely unrelated to the story you are working on at the moment.

For those problems the team can create *technical stories*: stories that are just about fixing a problem before it is too late. Those stories usually don't read like "As a <*somebody*>, I want <*something*> . . .," because they are invisible to users. You can either write "As the team, we want . . ." or abandon the "as a . . ." format this time.

The Product Owner can handle the story as any other story and take the team as the stakeholder. Even though the business value of technical stories may not be apparent immediately, there is of course business value in the long run; the Product Owner needs to balance the needs carefully.

Sometimes, a business stakeholder can become a stakeholder to the technical story too, because a feature she wants depends on the technical story. That usually makes its priority a lot more evident. The Product Owner should try to find business stakeholders as early as possible to be the champion of the technical story.

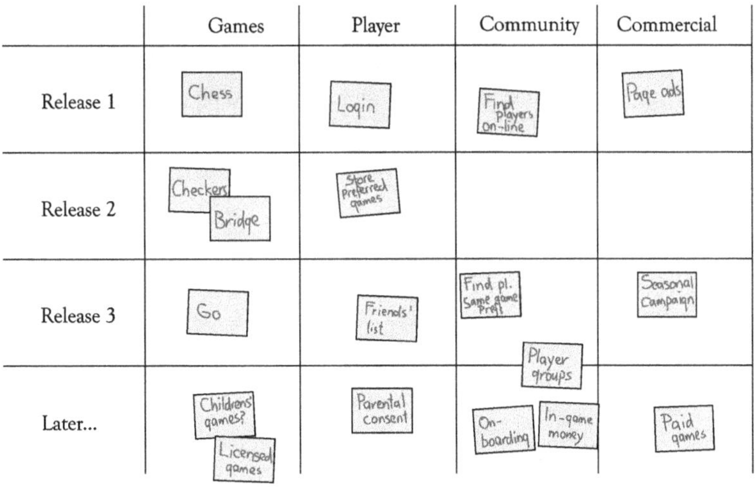

	Games	Player	Community	Commercial
Release 1	Chess	Login	Find players on-line	Page ads
Release 2	Checkers / Bridge	Store preferred games		
Release 3	Go	Friends' list	Find pl. Same game Prgt / Player groups	Seasonal Campaign
Later...	Childrens games? / Licensed games	Parental consent	On-boarding / In-game money	Paid games

Figure 10.3 A story map

Story Mapping

If your product backlog becomes large, just organizing it into a prioritized list may be hard. It might give a Product Owner the feeling that he or she is comparing apples and oranges when trying to decide between a technical story and a user story, or user stories for different audiences.

A tool that might help here is *Story Mapping*: Organize the backlog in two or more dimensions. For example, make each column represent a different theme or type of stories, in priority order from top to bottom. Now each row represents a sprint or a release. If there is too much in a release to be done, move down the item in one column to free up space. Work your way down through the grid until every release looks doable.

An example of a story map can be seen in Figure 10.3. This is a story map for an online web-based board games service. The map is organized in four themes: *Games*, *Player*, *Community*, and *Commercial*. In each column, stories or features are listed, in priority order from top to bottom. Now the top row shows a possible first release.

For the second release, work on more games was deemed more important than commercial features, so features from the other columns were moved down a bit.

There are different ways of story mapping possible. They all have in common that you use multiple dimensions to keep track of multiple properties of the work to do. You can find a lot more information about story mapping online.

10.2   The Scrum Master's Role

The Team was happily coding when Joe from Marketing hopped in.

"When does your sprint end? And is my story actually in it? Where is your Scrum board? Do you have your product backlog online somewhere? O, and can you reschedule your demos? I generally don't work on Fridays. Can I be in your retrospective?"

Sam sighed. "Get out of our team room!"

The Scrum Master is responsible for the Scrum process. Do you have a Scrum Master? If not, assign one.

10.2.1 What the Scrum Master Does

The Scrum Master's mundane tasks include making sure all the meetings happen, and possibly chair them: sizing meetings, sprint planning meetings, stand-up meetings, sprint demos, and retrospective meetings. Furthermore, he or she should make sure the Scrum board is there and is kept up to date, the burn-down chart is updated, and any impediments are cleared. But the responsibility of the Scrum Master goes a lot further.

By virtue of being responsible for the Scrum process, the Scrum Master must make sure that things happen. That doesn't mean the Scrum Master should *do* it all; after all, it's the team's process. But it is certainly helpful for the team if there is someone who keeps track of things.

The team concentrates on technical problems. And that's what they should do. The Scrum Master, on the other hand, should keep an eye on the process. Is everybody on time in meetings? Are people working together well? Are the good resolutions from the retrospective observed? Is the team performing well and improving? In other words, is the Scrum process working well?

If the Scrum Master sees anything that is not going well, he or she should make sure it is discussed in the team and a solution is found. Asking questions in the retrospective can be a very good way to make the team aware of something not going well; mentioning problems in the stand-up can also help. It is important to let the team as a whole come up with solutions. For example, just ordering the team to "be nicer to each other" is probably not going to work.

10.2.2 Say "No" to Disturbance

Apart from internal forces that prevent a good Scrum process, there are also external forces: stakeholders coming to the team to ask them questions or tell them to do things, managers that force work upon the team, or just a noisy or busy work environment. In fact, these are all impediments, but they might not be experienced as such.

Task-related blockers, like "my PC is broken" or "we still don't have the artwork," are easily recognized as impediments. More general things preventing you from doing work, like "Dean is constantly asking whether we are finished yet" or "Carol wants me to attend that half-day meeting every week," sometimes aren't.

These are impediments too, and they should be cleared. Again, the Scrum Master can be the right person to be extra keen on that kind of impediments.

10.2.3 Never Commit to Too Much Work

There can be a lot of pressure from stakeholders on the team to do certain stories. It can sometimes be hard to say "no" to people. Still, the team should never commit to more work than they think they can handle.

When the velocity of the team is reasonably well established, you just know you are not going to make it. So when you say "Oh well, we can look into it," you don't help the stakeholder at all. Instead of saying "no" right away, you effectively say "yes" now and "no" later.

The funny thing is that most stakeholders don't really care whether you say "no" or "yes," as long as that "yes" *really* is yes. (If the "no" is not really "no" they usually don't mind.) A real "yes" or "no" allows them to adjust their plans, and if you do what you promise then they can deliver what they promised.

And for yourself, it is actually easier to say "no" right away than to be forced to apologize later, because then the effect for the stakeholders (and thus the disappointment) is much larger.

10.3   The Team's Role

The Team has been coding like madmen, adding feature after feature at the speed of light … The stakeholders were never happier! But now the code base is a mess. Loose ends, unfinished business, quick hacks, ad-hoc design decisions … With Scrum you have to go so fast that you can never pay any attention to code cleanup!

So what's left for the team to do? Do the work, of course. But to be really successful at Scrum, there's a little bit more to it.

10.3.1 Just a Team, or a Scrum Team?

The key to Scrum (or any other method) is to work together very well. And for that, you need to talk together very well. Scrum allows you to do that and even prescribes that you do that, in planning meetings, stand-up meetings, and retrospectives. But it doesn't end there. You have to talk to each other *all the time*. Just imagine you are a rugby team: It's not just planning, half-time chat, and watching the video after the game, but it's also shouting and talking to help each other *during* the game.

And just like in a well-performing sports team, you will find out that after some time you just *know* what others are doing or how they are doing it. That is when the team members can completely trust each other with the job they are doing, and that is working together very well.

10.3.2 Be Responsible

If at any time, a team member is not doing what he or she said he or she would be doing, the trust in the team will be compromised. Also, if somebody sees that something is going wrong, but is not sharing it with the team, trust is not worth a lot.

As a team member, you are responsible for the success of the team, for the current sprint, and for the work you committed to. If you feel you cannot be responsible for a task, for example, because you lack the knowledge or you hate it too much, give it back. But don't pretend you're doing something that you are actually not doing.

10.3.3 Maximum Sustainable Pace

Sometimes, Scrum teams feel a lot of pressure they themselves created. The team becomes so much more efficient that they go into some sort of productivity frenzy, delivering as many new features as possible. But they value speed over good coding practices and honestly finishing things in a good way. They wear themselves out and build up defects in their code, all to get the highest possible velocity and try to deliver everything they committed to.

This is different from hyperproductivity, as they usually call the state a well-functioning Scrum team strives for. The difference is that they don't look forward how they can sustain this pace. Apart from the risk of burning out, if you value speed over good coding practices you leave your code base in a big mess. Although it is sometimes possible to accept *technical debt* to finish things faster, you have to pay back this debt, or fix these defects, to keep your code in a good shape. Else your technical debt will drag down your productivity in the long run.

Refactoring, improving, and tidying up is an integral part of all the work you do. If you get the balance right between caring for old code and writing new code, your code base will continuously improve while you are delivering new features at the same time. Your pace of development will allow you to finish stories quickly, without leaving problems that will need to be solved later.

The right balance is usually called the *maximum sustainable pace*. Work as fast as you can, but not faster. The "waveform" of sprints will make sure you can keep up a fast pace for a long time.

Kaizen

Originally the Japanese word *kaizen* means nothing else than "improvement," but after Toyota's success in lean production, it got a more specific taste to it.

Kaizen now implies small experiments that lead to small changes in a process that can be made into a standard when they are successful. Most of all, it needs to be applied continuously. Many small improvements will lead to a much better process. That is why kaizen is usually translated to "continuous improvement."

10.3.4 Continuous Improvement

Things are always changing: New projects arrive, new people are hired, new things become important. It is up to the team to try to change for the better.

As a team, you should always try to improve. "Inspect and adapt" is the motto of Scrum: See what works well and keep on doing it, see what causes problems and avoid it in the future. But also try out new things, and if you like it, keep it. Don't try to improve by completely changing the way you work; that is very time consuming and will also get rid of good things. Just try to continuously improve small things. You will be surprised how effective that can be.

10.3.5 Keep the Team Together

The team cannot improve if the team changes constantly. If people together can accomplish more than those people alone, that doesn't happen just like that; it takes time for a team to perform better than the individuals. Team members have to get used to each other and to each other's way of working, before they can work together well.

All this investment is wasted if the team is disbanded. In an organization using Scrum, resource management should never be based on the availability of *persons*, but always on the priority of work and the velocity of *teams*. The team as a whole can perform at a certain pace; the availability of a single person is largely irrelevant.

Actually, well-performing Scrum teams sometimes don't see a drop in velocity if a team member is on holiday for a full sprint. In the long run, the velocity will go down, but in the short term the team can make up for the lower availability, which clearly shows that the team is more important for release planning than the individuals.

10.4   Scrum: Getting It Right

"Now The Team is doing Scrum!"

—The Team

There is a lot of wisdom in Scrum. All the simple elements of the methodology work together to bring out the best in teams, continuously. If you leave out one element, you're missing out on an opportunity to do better.

The only way to make Scrum work is by doing it very well. Pay attention to all the little details. Have a Product Owner who knows what his or her role is, and have a Scrum Master who knows what he or she is doing. Have a team that communicates well and knows how to improve. The Scrum team will perform better and become more and more autonomous. Trust in the team will grow: the team will really have created the power to do things well. Agile teaches us that the team should be empowered, but in the end, the team will empower itself.

10.5   Have Fun!

There is one thing that can't be repeated enough: When done well, Scrum is a lot of fun. If the team grows to a level of autonomy that makes them well performing, dependable and trusted, they enjoy work that is interesting, fun, and fulfilling.

So have fun!

Bibliography

Ambler, S. 2002. *Agile Modeling: Effective Practices for eXtreme Programming and the Unified Process.* New York, NY: Wiley.

Beaumont, S. 2009. "Flow to READY, Iterate to DONE." *Xebia Blog.* July 4. http://blog.xebia.com/flow-to-ready-iterate-to-done

Beck, K. 1999. *eXtreme Programming explained: Embrace Change.* Boston: Addison-Wesley.

Cohn, M. 2005. *Agile Estimating and Planning.* Upper Saddle River, NJ: Prentice Hall PTR.

Cohn, M. 2009. *Succeeding with Agile: Software Development Using Scrum.* Boston: Addison-Wesley.

Covey, S. R. 2004. *The 7 Habits of Highly Effective People: Powerful Lessons in Personal Change.* New York, NY: Simon & Schuster.

Covey, S. R. 2005. *The 8th Habit: From Effectiveness to Greatness.* New York: Free Press.

Derby, E., and D. Larsen. 2012. *Agile Retrospectives: Making Good Teams Great.* Raleigh, NC: The Pragmatic Bookshelf.

Hunt, A., and D. Thomas. 1999. *The Pragmatic Programmer: From Journeyman to Master.* Boston: Addison-Wesley.

Kniberg, H. 2007. *Scrum and XP from the Trenches: How We Do Scrum.* lulu.com.

Langr, J., T. Ottinger, and S. Pfalzer. 2011. *Agile in a Flash: Speed-Learning Agile Software Development.* Raleigh, NC: Pragmatic Bookshelf.

Martin, R. C., J. O. Coplien, K. Wampler, J. W. Grenning, B. L. Schuchert, J. Langr, T. R. Ottinger, and M. C. Feathers. 2009. *Clean Code: A Handbook of Agile Software Craftsmanship.* Upper Saddle River, NJ: Prentice Hall.

Poppendieck, M. 2002. "Lean Construction." *LeanEssays.* March 5. http://www.leanessays.com/2002/03/lean-construction.html.

Schwaber, K., and M. Beedle. 2001. *Agile Software Development with Scrum.* Upper Saddle River, NJ: Prentice Hall PTR.

Schwaber, K., and J. Sutherland. 2017. "The Scrum Guide." *The Scrum Guide*, November 1. http://www.scrumguides.org/.

Tuckman, B. W. 1965. "Developmental Sequence in Small Groups." *Psychological Bulletin* 63 (6): 384–99.

Tuckman, B. W., and M. A. C. Jensen. 1977. "Stages of Small-Group Development Revisited." *Group & Organization Studies* 2 (4): 419–27.

Index

OTHER TITLES IN OUR PORTFOLIO AND PROJECT MANAGEMENT COLLECTION

Timothy J. Kloppenborg, *Editor*

- *Improving Executive Sponsorship of Projects: A Holistic Approach* by Dawne Chandler and Payson Hall
- *Co-Create: Harnessing the Human Element in Project Management* by Steve Martin
- *Financing and Managing Projects, Volume I: A Guide for Executives and Professionals* by Nand L. Dhameja, Ashok Panjwani, and Vijay Aggarwal
- *Financing and Managing Projects, Volume II: A Guide for Executives and Professionals* by Nand L. Dhameja, Ashok Panjwani, and Vijay Aggarwal
- *Agile Management: The Fast and Flexible Approach to Continuous Improvement and Innovation in Organizations* by Mike Hoogveld
- *A Practical Guide for Holistic Project Management* by Lex van der Heijden
- *Project Management and Leadership Challenges-Volume I: Applying Project Management Principles for Organizational Transformation* by M. Aslam Mirza
- *Innoliteracy: From Design Thinking to Tangible Change* by Steinar Valade-Amland
- *Project Management and Leadership Challenges, Volume II: Understanding Human Factors And Workplace Environment* by M. Aslam Mirza
- *Project Management and Leadership Challenges, Volume III: Respecting Diversity, Building Team Meaningfulness, and Growing Into Leadership Roles* by M. Aslam Mirza
- *Why Projects Fail: Nine Laws for Success* by Tony Martyr
- *Project Management and Leadership Challenges, Volume IV: Agility in Project Management and Collaboration* by M. Aslam Mirza

Announcing the Business Expert Press Digital Library

Concise e-books business students need for classroom and research

This book can also be purchased in an e-book collection by your library as

- a one-time purchase,
- that is owned forever,
- allows for simultaneous readers,
- has no restrictions on printing, and
- can be downloaded as PDFs from within the library community.

Our digital library collections are a great solution to beat the rising cost of textbooks. E-books can be loaded into their course management systems or onto students' e-book readers. The **Business Expert Press** digital libraries are very affordable, with no obligation to buy in future years. For more information, please visit **www.businessexpertpress.com/librarians**. To set up a trial in the United States, please email **sales@businessexpertpress.com**.